Foreword

The ability to deliver construction projects to the required quality more quickly is an issue that all those involved in the construction industry should address to ensure greater satisfaction of clients and their end-users.

Faster delivery is generally the result of an integrated approach from the whole supply chain, to which each member brings specific expertise in the ordered selection and adoption of a particular solution to meet client needs. Faster construction on site can be an important requirement of the delivery process.

This guide is aimed at clients, designers, contractors and suppliers working on projects where faster delivery is essential. This may be as a result of market pressures, funding pressures or operational pressures – in each case there is a clear need to provide the chosen facility more quickly than would traditionally be possible.

The key message of the guidance is that the achievement of substantially faster construction on site is a supply chain management issue. It will be the outcome of rational collective decision-making within the project team by the application of a structured approach in the whole project process. The greatest opportunities for improving the speed of construction on site come in the early stages of the process. However, it is recognised that there are opportunities to influence construction time throughout the process. Early involvement of specialist contractors and suppliers in the design development is particularly helpful, as is greater use of prefabrication, pre-assembly and modularisation.

Section 1 provides background information to the subject and sets out the approach adopted for the guidance. Section 2 describes a selection process for methods and materials, together with some tools to allow members of the team to compare alternative options. Section 3 presents the project process in three principal phases, where the leading emphasis is: definition of the project (planning-led), design of the project (design-led) and implementation of the project (construction-led), respectively. Section 4 provides support to the selection of methods and materials, with key points for achieving faster construction sequences, more specific ideas for particular areas of work, additional case studies and further sources of information.

Sections 1 and 2 should be read in full. This is to gain a deeper understanding of the philosophy of selecting methods and materials to achieve faster construction on site. The reader can then dip into the relevant parts of Sections 3 and 4 to obtain specific advice. Section 3 addresses the project process and Section 4 provides supporting information on each part of the construction sequence for a typical building or structure.

Acknowledgements

This book results from the work carried out under CIRIA Research Project 589. It was prepared by Ove Arup Partnership Ltd under contract to CIRIA. The project supervisor was Allan Delves and the principal authors were Allan Delves, Roger Drayton and Tony Sheehan. The illustrations were prepared by Fred English. CIRIA's research manager for the project was David Churcher.

Funding

The research project was funded by the Department of the Environment, Transport and the Regions (DETR) through its Partners in Innovation scheme, the Institution of Civil Engineers (ICE) Research & Development Enabling Fund, CIRIA's Core Programme and from a contribution-in-kind from Ove Arup Partnership Ltd.

Project steering group

A steering group, established by CIRIA to advise on technical content, guided the research. This comprised:

Mark Sewell (chairman)	Balfour Beatty Major Projects
Ian Bolton	Gifford & Partners
John Caves	London Underground
John Fielding	Maunsell Ltd
Peter Hansford	Redbourn Consulting (representing ICE)
Rod Howes	South Bank University
Martin Lockwood	Davis Langdon Consultancy (representing DETR)
Neil Moore	Balfour Beatty Major Projects
Justin Nicholls	Foster & Partners
Bram Paton	Taylor Woodrow

Contributions to the project were also made by:

Tony Brown	Heery International
John Findlay	Stent Foundations Ltd
Richard Jeffcoate	BAA plc
Terence Mallinson	Timber Industry Alliance

The questionnaire

The following responded to the questionnaire issued as part of the research project:

Ian Bolton	Gifford and Partners
John Caves	London Underground Ltd
Graeme Forrest-Brown	Maunsell Ltd
Rod Howes	Faculty of the Built Environment
Neil Moore	Balfour Beatty Major Projects
Bram Paton	Taylor Woodrow Construction
Peter Jones	Construction Best Practice Programme
Charles McBeath	Whitby Bird & Partners
Sue Hobbs	Construction Best Practice Programme
Peter Thompson	Slough Estates
Glenn Hawkins	Building Services Research & Information Association
Gary Connolly	Crown House Engineering Ltd
Chris Sneath	CJ Bartley
Mike Downing	Trent Concrete
Brian Hicks	Colas Ltd
Alan McGibney	Civil and Marine Slag Cement Company
Peter Sehmi	Lafarge-Redland Aggregates
Cliff Fudge	H&H Celcon
S E Bell	Marshalls
Graham Gedge	Ove Arup Partnership Ltd
Adrian Jackson-Robbins	Davies Langdon Consultancy
R H Deacon	Bovis Construction Limited
J M Pritchard	Tarmac Building
Justin Nicholls	Foster and Partners
Martin Southcott	Reinforced Concrete Council
Jeff Richards	Dow Corning

Ove Arup Partnership Ltd and CIRIA would like to express their sincere thanks to all those who have contributed to the book.

CIRIA and the authors gratefully acknowledge the support of these funding organisations and the technical help and advice provided by the members of the steering group. Contributions do not imply that individual funders necessarily endorse all views expressed in published outputs.

Recent Government reorganisation has meant that DETR responsibilities have been moved variously to the Department of Trade and Industry (DTI), the Department for the Environment, Food and Rural Affairs (DEFRA), and the Department for Transport, Local Government and the Regions (DTLR). References made to the DETR in this publication should be read in this context.

For clarification, readers should contact the Department of Trade and Industry.

Contents

1.1 The need for faster construction

Clients often demand faster construction so as to benefit from early completion of projects. Although there are notable examples where fast construction has been achieved, the consensus is that the construction industry has not been entirely successful in meeting clients' expectations. This is primarily due to a fragmented industry, in which design is often separated from the construction activities. Traditional practices are proving inadequate, to the point where either they can no longer achieve the desired delivery time, or, if projects are forced to meet the programme, they do not provide the required quality and long-term performance. If faster construction is needed, the level of attainment of the targets is an essential part of assessing the overall performance of the construction industry in meeting client needs.

The publication specifically addressing these issues was *Constructing the team*, by Sir Michael Latham (1994), which set out 30 recommendations to improve the construction industry's performance. Among these were proposals to improve the integration of the processes and achieve reduced cost and time for project delivery, including on-site construction times.

The publication *Rethinking construction*, by the Egan task force, aimed to build on the recommendations of *Constructing the team*. It stated that, to achieve the targets, radical changes were required to the current processes for delivery of projects.

Achievement of faster construction on site is an integral part of implementing the overall recommendations of these important publications.

This guide is designed to be used by all members of the project team and supply chains throughout the project process. The guidance will help users achieve faster construction on site by selecting appropriate methods and materials, while maintaining the required levels of quality and safety, and taking account of environmental and sustainability issues.

1.2 What is faster construction?

Broadly, "faster construction" means achieving a shorter overall project timescale to meet a client's needs compared to that achieved by adopting a traditional approach. It is important to pay attention to the activities that comprise each stage of the project process, from briefing to completion, as well as to the relationship between the stages. The project team should demonstrate clear commitment to making the stages in the process more efficient and effective. Good management practice is essential to operate clear, simple systems that achieve timely decisions and actions from all parties in a co-ordinated team to achieve the defined goals. In-depth comment on this subject is outside the scope of this publication.

This book concentrates on the achievement of shorter timescales for the actual construction on site for the structure or facility through the selection of construction methods and materials.

The project team can generally achieve faster construction on site through the preparation of appropriate designs and the selection of the right methods and materials. It should implement the following, either individually or, preferably, in combination, depending on the project requirements:

- an increase in production rates (including reducing errors, waste and rework)
- reduction in cycle times for repetitive activities
- introduction of parallel working
- use of prefabrication, pre-assembly and modularisation.

The optimum selection of construction methods, materials and suppliers is an important part of improving on-site construction times. In general, the design team and specialist contractors should both be involved at the earliest appropriate stage of the project process and should address selection at each stage to achieve the solutions for faster construction on site. This approach should not be constrained by traditional contractual arrangements. The design team and the client both need to be able to give timely decisions.

Constructing faster on site will almost certainly have an impact on other criteria. For example, there will probably be a greater need to review cost carefully, to raise safety concerns and to set quality, environmental and sustainability standards. It is important, therefore, to identify and focus on those activities that are critical to achieving the target programme, to ensure uncertainty is removed from the programme's critical path. It is important to maintain consistency, so that gain in one activity is not lost later in the sequence.

1.3 Objective of this guidance

The objective of this guide is to provide advice and encourage creative thinking to assist clients, designers, contractors and suppliers select appropriate methods and materials for faster construction on site. The book:

- addresses the whole project process from briefing to completion
- promotes early interaction between clients, designers, contractors and suppliers
- advises on the selection process for appropriate methods and materials
- focuses on the issues to be addressed and on the provision of solutions
- provides guidance, supplemented by examples and other references.

1.4 The project process

The project process should enable the client's brief to be developed in a way that achieves the overall project objectives. Design development should take place throughout the process, progressing from general issues to specific details in an ordered manner. Various procurement methods can be incorporated interactively to meet the specific demands of the project. The project process is shown diagrammatically in Figure 1.1.

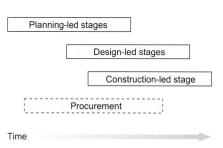

Time

Figure 1.1 Project process

1.4.1 Planning-led stages

Briefing

The briefing stage is the first and principal opportunity for the client to set out the project objectives to meet business needs. The briefing activities develop the scope and functional information and set the boundaries, including the time targets. This stage effectively continues up to the end of the feasibility stage. Although the possible need for faster construction on site is discussed at this point, selection of construction methods and materials is not a major consideration. For this reason, briefing stage activities are not addressed further in this guide.

Procurement

Procurement activities take place alongside the sequential development of the project process. The various methods of procurement interact with, and relate to, each stage, depending on the approach adopted. Methods of procurement vary widely. Some involve contractors and specialists at the earliest stages, while in others tendering takes place after the detail design stage, when many of the project parameters have already been set and to which construction must conform. The former approach has proved more successful in achieving faster construction on site and is more in tune with the principles of *Rethinking construction* **(see 3.2.1).**

Feasibility

The feasibility stage explores the options that could meet the business needs and other objectives. The preferred solution is chosen once it has been established that it is functionally, technically and financially feasible. This stage most likely determines the need for faster construction on site. It is assumed that this applies as a requirement for the remainder of this guide **(see 3.2.2).**

1.4.2 Design-led stages

Concept design

The preferred solution is developed in terms of architecture, structural form, engineering and internal design. Options for the major physical and engineering systems are studied and preferred solutions selected. The methods of manufacture and construction, and the materials, under consideration should all be consistent with the desired time-frame for completion. Contractors and specialist suppliers or advisers should preferably be involved at this stage to advise on achieving faster construction on site **(see 3.3.1).**

Scheme design

At this stage, the general arrangements are developed and co-ordinated design takes place, fixing the major design systems and elements. The level of co-ordination should be sufficient to enable cost, safety, quality, environmental, sustainability and operational performance to be predicted accurately. Planning takes place for the manufacture and methods of construction, together with integration of the appropriate materials and products for achieving faster construction on site **(see 3.3.2).**

Detailed production design

Production information is prepared at this stage. Consultants, contractors and suppliers detail all components of the project and finalise plans for the manufacture and assembly operations, including details of the materials to be used **(see 3.3.3).**

1.4.3 Construction-led stage

Construction site assembly and installation

At the construction stage all the plans for manufacture, assembly and on-site construction are implemented. Work is carried out in accordance with the design and programmes set during the design and procurement processes **(see 3.4.1).**

1.5 Structure of this guidance

This guide is structured to promote thought and provide advice on the achievement of faster construction on site. It centres on the selection process for methods and materials in relation to the project process stages from feasibility through to completion. The book is divided into the following sections:

1 Introduction

- The section introduces both the topic and this book (this section). The section should be read in full.

2 How to select construction methods and materials

- This describes the selection process, which is seen as common for the selection of methods and materials at all stages as the project develops. It covers the techniques that may be employed to ensure optimum selection for faster construction on site, and should be read in full.

3 Achieving faster construction on site

- This provides advice on, and examples of, achieving faster construction on site by considering methods and materials at each stage of the project process, taking into account the procurement method adopted. It will be of most benefit if the guidance is applied to the earliest stages of a project. However, some benefit can still be gained if the principles are applied in the later stages, although there is less opportunity to achieve radical improvements. This section can be referred to at any stage of the project process.

4 Supporting information

- This provides supplementary guidance for particular elements of the work, or the organisation of the construction site as a whole. It also includes more detailed examples, useful points of further contact and additional references. This section can be referred to for advice as required.

For ease of reference, each part of Section 3 is indicated along the outer edges of the pages, coded in accordance with the structure shown in Figure 1.2.

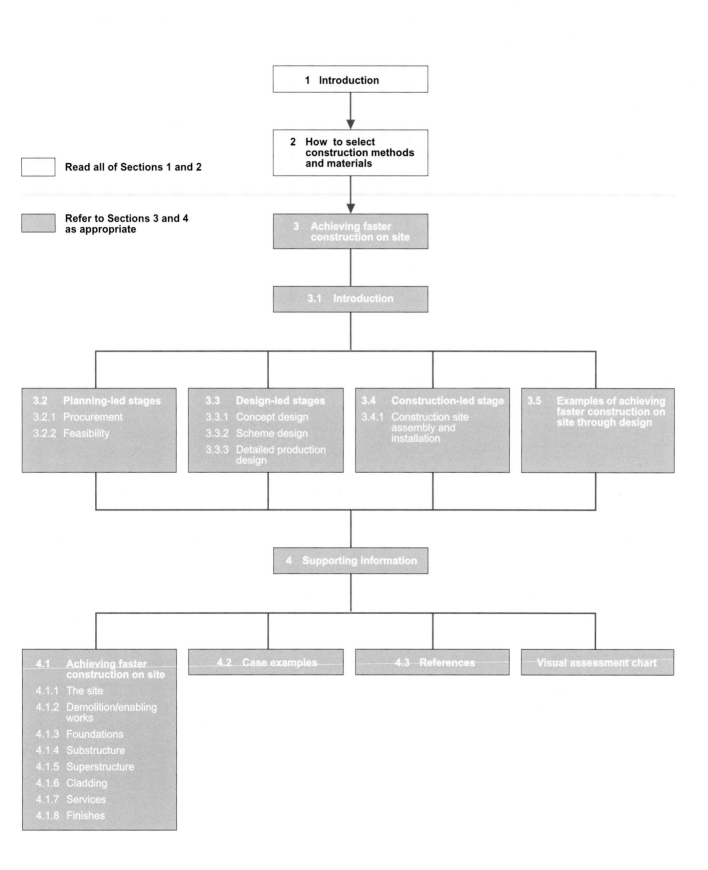

1 Introduction

2 How to select construction methods and materials

Read all of Sections 1 and 2

Refer to Sections 3 and 4 as appropriate

3 Achieving faster construction on site

3.1 Introduction

3.2 Planning-led stages
3.2.1 Procurement
3.2.2 Feasibility

3.3 Design-led stages
3.3.1 Concept design
3.3.2 Scheme design
3.3.3 Detailed production design

3.4 Construction-led stage
3.4.1 Construction site assembly and installation

3.5 Examples of achieving faster construction on site through design

4 Supporting information

4.1 Achieving faster construction on site
4.1.1 The site
4.1.2 Demolition/enabling works
4.1.3 Foundations
4.1.4 Substructure
4.1.5 Superstructure
4.1.6 Cladding
4.1.7 Services
4.1.8 Finishes

4.2 Case examples

4.3 References

Visual assessment chart

Figure 1.2 Diagrammatic contents list

2.1 Introduction

Selecting methods and materials to contribute to faster construction on site should be by a logical process that results in a preferred choice for implementation. Before starting the process, it is essential to understand the project-specific needs and objectives. The available options can then be assessed and the choice made.

Selecting appropriate materials and methods for construction requires consideration of numerous options, so there is ample scope for mistakes, confusion and delay. The selection process should be integrated into the development of the design. The selection should be carried out in parallel with, and in recognition of the requirements for, other project criteria, such as aesthetics, structural capacity, durability, whole-life costs and serviceability. Advice from specialists in the early stages is important, as is access to the necessary skills for assessing and choosing methods and materials.

In the evaluation process, a balance has to be achieved between the flexible elements of a project: time, cost and scope. Similarly, a balance has to be struck between the much less flexible elements: health and safety, environmental impact, quality and sustainability.

Each team will have its own way of selecting the "best" methods and materials for the project, and there is no single right method. Nevertheless, it is possible to propose a selection process that is visible and accessible to all members of the project team. There is a constant need to balance methods, materials and programme.

There is also a need to recognise that some factors override others and cannot be compromised (eg health and safety), whereas others (eg colour and durability) vary according to project requirements and budget.

It is important to review and reflect on decisions at each stage of the project process, and to record the thinking behind each decision. In this way, everyone in the project team can understand the reasons for selecting particular methods and materials (see 3.2–3.4). The aim must be to minimise changes as far as possible, or at least to make the logic behind key decisions as transparent as possible so that future changes are made in the correct context (see 4.1).

The selection process consists of four main activities:

- identification of key issues
- listing of boundaries and assumptions
- assessing and choosing the preferred option
- implementing the chosen option.

Techniques are available that allow balanced comparison of a large number of factors to be compared in a balanced way. Their use can help ensure that the comparisons are reliable and easily understood. This section addresses the selection process and highlights a review and recording technique for use in most project circumstances (see 2.3).

2.2 The selection process

Table 2.1 below describes a proposed selection process for construction methods and materials to achieve faster construction on site. This process is included later in the guide in the sections giving advice for each of the project stages. Table 2.2 gives examples of the selection process.

ACTIVITY	STEP	EXPLANATION
Identify key issues	**Identify context**	Understand the circumstances of the particular needs. What are the objectives?
	Identify issues	What are the major aspects of the context that will govern the direction of the ongoing process?
List boundaries and assumptions	**List constraints/ opportunities**	What are the boundaries of the context and issues?
	List assumptions	What assumptions have been made or are necessary to adequately simplify the choice of options?
Assess and choose preferred option	**Assess and select options**	Are the options selected appropriate to the context objectives? Has the best use of innovation and technology been included?
	Evaluate options	How are the options to be compared and the priority decided?
	Choose preferred option	How is the best option to be chosen? What are the criteria? Are changes possible?
Implement chosen option	**Progress to solution**	How should the option development progress to implementation?

Table 2.1   Selection process

Key Activity	Building at Feasibility Stage	Civil Engineering Structure at Concept Stage	Services System Project at Concept Stage
Identify key issues		IDENTIFY CONTEXT	
	The supermarket needs to be open by 15 October to catch the Christmas trade and therefore is a fast-build programme	Motorway sign/signal gantries to be installed to avoid significant motorway or lane closures of new in-use motorway	Sprinkler tank farm for high-fire-load factory to move to new location to avoid new adjacent railway alignment about to pass the site
		IDENTIFY ISSUES	
	Obtaining planning consent will compress the available programme for detailed design and construction	1 Gantries span live in-use carriageways 2 Aesthetics 3 Functionality	To work towards sprinkler relocation end date, negotiate with local authority to confirm no planning application requirement
List boundaries and assumptions		LIST CONSTRAINTS AND OPPORTUNITIES	
	A shorter design period will favour the selection of the standardised components and offer faster construction	1 Rolling-block lane closures 2 No motorway or lane closures 3 Inspection, maintenance or modification 4 Future proofing 5 Design standards	1 Existing business ongoing 2 Fixed early end date means design for faster construction 3 Client pre-ordering of long lead-in plant items 4 Satisfy sprinkler regulations
		LIST ASSUMPTIONS	
	1 No specials 2 No overseas sourcing 3 Cost is a secondary issue	1 Flexibility of system 2 No lane closures > 10 minutes	1 Standard plant and equipment to be specified 2 Negotiate for main contractor 3 Large contingency
Assess and choose preferred option		ASSESS AND SELECT OPTIONS	
	1 Timber 2 Precast concrete 3 Steel	1 Cost 2 Speed of erection 3 Maintenance 4 Extent of consultation	1 Type of water tank to be used 2 Requirements for diesel or electric pumps 3 Requirement for standby generator 4 Housing construction material
		EVALUATE OPTIONS	
	Score options most highly on: 1 Number of workfaces 2 Speed of hand-over to following trades 3 Readily available designs/material	Score options most highly on: 1 Cost 2 Speed of erection 3 Maintenance 4 Extent of consultation	Score options most highly on: 1 Tank installation 2 Easy/safe plant access 3 Early commissioning 4 Early housing for plant
		CHOOSE PREFERRED OPTION	
	Precast concrete gives overall faster solution	Open truss gives maximum design flexibility providing minimum (fast) erection time and easy maintenance	1 Sectional circular water tank 2 Electric pumps on main power 3 Standby diesel generator
Implement chosen option		PROGRESS TO SOLUTION	
	Need to consider the detailed erection sequence/method for faster option	1 Use of standard elements 2 Efficient foundation design 3 Long-life paint systems	1 Generator extra cost reduces contingency 2 Need for tight control of spending while maintaining faster programme

Table 2.2   Selection process – examples

2.3 A review and recording technique

2.3.1 Introduction

When all the specialists, materials suppliers and contractors engaged on a project are brought in as early as practicable a common approach to selection should be developed. This is to enable everyone in the project team to understand the context and the issues of historical decisions and to recognise the need to develop appropriate justifications for change.

The project team and the specialist suppliers are always likely to have different priorities. It is important, however:

- to bring these priorities into the open
- for all to highlight their primary needs up front
- to come to a balanced decision regarding the preferred choice.

The team should draw up a list of important factors to be considered and agreed as the desirable characteristics of the methods/materials to be used on the project. Individual methods or materials under consideration in the selection process can then be compared against this list. There is a risk that team members might miss an important criterion, but the effects of this can be minimised by ongoing review. The team might choose to assess each method or material from "bad" to "good" on an arbitrary scale of 1 to 10. It should take care with this ranking. Generally, a low cost would be good and therefore rank higher than a high cost. Similarly, high strength would usually be good and rank higher than a low strength. However, the appropriate ranking for each factor varies from project to project, so the exercise should be carried out separately for each project. The ranking is only valuable in this context for definitions made by the project team, so the figures do not need to relate directly to absolute values of strength, stiffness, speed of construction etc.

A typical list of criteria, with weighting and ranking (each rated from 1 to 10 – poor to good) for a comparison of materials, is shown in Table 2.3.

For a particular project the appropriate list of criteria can be developed and the rankings and weighting applied as appropriate.

Criterion	Weighting	Material A	Material B	Material C
Safety	10	1	4	7
Durability	9	6	6	8
Initial cost	8	4	7	4
Life-cycle cost	7	3	5	6
Appearance	6	4	6	2
Strength	5	5	5	6
Stiffness	4	3	6	7
Ease of installation	3	8	6	4
Availability	2	6	5	6
Strength gain	1	5	7	7

Table 2.3 Example of comparative ranking of three materials for ten criteria

If individual factors are assessed in isolation, there is a risk that one factor will swamp all the others. Low cost, for example, should be compared with speed of construction or expected component life before it is used as the justification for selecting a method or material. The process can result in an unwieldy list in which it is difficult to recognise the significant trends, strengths or weaknesses of the options.

Using a visual assessment technique is one way of helping overcome this difficulty. Criteria are arranged in order of weighting clockwise around a circle, and the various options for methods or materials can be compared more holistically.

Using this method for the factors described in Table 2.3 produces the chart shown in Figure 2.1.

The technique conveys a feel for the various options and allows them to be weighed up in a balanced way. As the factors are arranged in order of importance (weighting) around the chart, the material showing best in this segment should be the preferred choice. In the example above, Material C looks the best overall choice, but it is not ideal. If appearance were critical, for example, Material B might prove to be the superior choice.

Minimum performance standards for these factors can be defined if desired, with the minimum required performance for each factor highlighted in turn. This can also be plotted on the visual assessment charts. If any proposed choices fall short of these minimum standards, they should be eliminated.

Visual assessment provides a means of recognising the key aims of the selection, and of selecting methods and materials against these aims. Should alternative

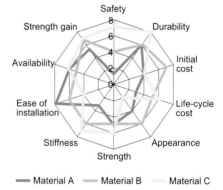

Figure 2.1 Visual assessment – comparison of three materials

methods or materials be considered at a later stage of the project process, visual assessment provides a safety net, ensuring that the project team's initial intentions are preserved when the alternative methods or materials are adopted.

The use of assessment charts in the decision-making process allows the project team to:

- compare the benefits and weaknesses of different criteria associated with methods and materials
- identify the benefits of unique methods or new materials (such that they are not unthinkingly substituted by cheaper alternatives at a late stage).

The following sections discuss the use of assessment charts in the selection of methods and materials. The Construction Best Practice Programme highlights key performance indicators for projects, and it will be useful at an early stage of a project to make comparisons against these indicators.

It is also possible to use these charts to collate information on project progress and to compare this with agreed targets and objectives (see 2.3.4).

2.3.2 Selection of methods

At an early stage in the design development, the project team has to review a wide range of construction methods. The team needs to reduce and refine these choices into a single approach. The approach should be one that team members consider the most suitable way forward within that project's constraints. Thereafter, the aim is to map the process, recognise key steps and optimise these to realise faster construction times on site.

The visual assessment technique allows the team to compare characteristics for method selection on a single chart throughout the project process. See Figure 2.2

Figure 2.2 Visual assessment – comparison of four methods

From this analysis, it is possible to see that Method 4 achieves faster construction time, with fewer defects and greatest safety. The likelihood of these advantages being outweighed by the reduced predictability of cost and time will need to be discussed and, if Method 4 is chosen, these elements should be subject to careful review as the project proceeds.

The descriptions used are examples only. If other factors are identified as important, they should be highlighted at an early stage and retained on the chart so that all recognise their critical role throughout the project.

2.3.3 Selection of materials

For materials, a consistent list of criteria should be considered at various stages (eg safety, durability, value, strength, stiffness, sustainability, buildability). As the project evolves, the selection process should become more specific and focused on products. There will be a gradual shift from broad consideration of a number of materials to detailed consideration of combinations of products.

The focus should change as the project proceeds as below:

The visual assessment technique allows the team to compare several characteristics on a single chart throughout the project process. See Figure 2.3

Figure 2.3 Visual assessment – comparison of two materials

Introducing change without considering the consequences can prevent the ideal of zero-defect buildings being realised. An example is the substitution of cheap materials at a late stage in the construction process without a full understanding of the material needs. Use of these charts helps ensure that all understand the importance of the many factors in the materials selection process.

As with methods, the above criteria are indicative. An appropriate list can be developed for each project that highlights characteristics such as speed of construction, strength gain, drying-out time etc.

2.3.4 Progress monitoring

It is possible to collate information on project progress and compare this with agreed targets at that time. Individual factors can be compared with targets on a linear scale. See Figure 2.4

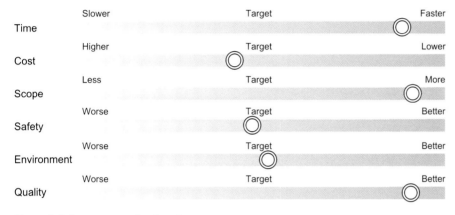

Figure 2.4 Progress monitoring shown on linear scale

Assessment charts provide a straightforward means of combining this information on a single diagram. See Figure 2.5

Figure 2.5 Progress monitoring shown on a visual assessment chart

The chart illustrates that the project is running ahead of time, with good quality and acceptable attention to safety and the environment. However, the current cost is worse than the predicted target value. The rankings 0 to 10 are related to the degree ahead or behind target for each objective.

A large-scale assessment chart for use by the reader on project work is given at the end of this book – Visual assessment chart template.

3.1 Introduction

The target of faster construction on site should be set at the earliest stages of the project process if it is to contribute to the client's overall objectives. Planning throughout the process is essential and success depends on use of appropriate specialist advice at each stage.

The most important contributor to faster construction on site is integration of the design and construction planning functions with specialist advice. This allows development of the optimum solutions for the on-site assembly works within the time constraints and is shown diagrammatically in Figure 3.1.

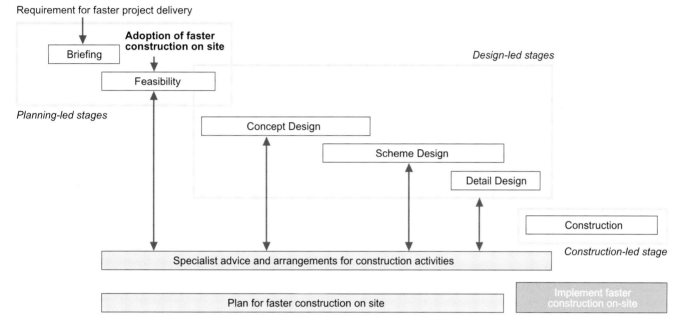

Figure 3.1 Achieving faster construction on site

The headings in this section follow the main phases of the project process described in Section 1.4 – ie planning-led, design-led and construction-led.

Each phase contains the respective stage of the project process and is addressed separately (except briefing). The design-led stages are presented as advice sheets in a common layout:

- Part 1: (a) Purpose and (b) Planning faster construction on site

- Part 2: Selection at the particular project stage

- Part 3: Selection of construction methods and materials

- Part 4: Stage summary.

This approach allows for an ordered progression from one stage to the next, with each involving planning, selection, review and summary. The advice sheets can be referred to at the appropriate stage of the project process (**see 3.2.1**).

Briefing is not addressed in further detail in this guide. Procurement is addressed as the opening Section 3.2.1.

3.2 Planning-led stages

3.2.1 Procurement

Procurement is the management arrangement by which a project is realised. The method chosen to achieve this varies according to the client's needs and objectives. Differing approaches to procurement reflect differing management arrangements. These involve the fundamental supply elements of the industry: designers, contractors, equipment and material suppliers, specialist contractors etc.

The procurement activities take place alongside the sequential development of the design stages as they move from feasibility to detail design and onto construction. The procedures and activities of the various procurement methods inter-relate at each stage and depend on the approach taken.

Procurement systems fall into three main categories:

- traditional contracting
- design-and-build
- management type.

Each method has its strengths and weaknesses and interacts with the project process at a particular stage. Success depends on the selection of the appropriate method to meet project needs. Clients vary: some carry out just one major project very occasionally, while others undertake large capital works regularly. The procurement arrangements that need to be made vary accordingly, because they are governed by the client's knowledge and previous experience of construction works.

Fast-track construction can be adopted for any of the above methods. It involves overlapping design and construction to reduce the duration of the project, but it does not necessarily decrease the time spent on construction on site. Unless design and construction are integrated, the approach can build-in many inefficiencies.

All current methods of procurement involve some division of work into packages, either for specialist trades or for suppliers. While this facilitates control of the specialist elements of projects, it does not constitute a holistic approach for project delivery and can create inefficiencies at interfaces, unless they are particularly well managed.

Faster construction on site should be stated as a prime objective to meet the client's needs from the start of the project, so that the best procurement method to achieve this aim can be selected. To obtain appropriate advice early in the project, options for methods and materials need to be incorporated into the design considerations as early as possible. Contractors are usually specialists in construction methods and materials. Suppliers have the best knowledge of their particular products or components. Clearly, it is essential to have the early commitment of those providing the advice. However, it is neither appropriate nor practical to involve all specialist suppliers into the design team at the start of a project (see 4.2).

The benefit of partnering and framework agreements becomes apparent when good quality advice is regularly being sought from specialists. Agreed quality approaches can then be established and developed, particularly in the early ordering of selected materials, development of off-site fabrication and modularisation. Alliancing allows these principles to be incorporated for clients that undertake capital works less frequently.

Table 3.1 below summarises the main advantages and disadvantages of each of the procurement methods mentioned above in relation to faster construction on site. It also shows where each method interacts with the project process to provide maximum benefit.

| Procurement method | Faster construction on site | | |
	Pros	Cons	Interaction with the project process
Traditional contracting*	Client able to dictate parameters	• Contract parameters set • Construction has to fit	Tender and construction stages
Design and build*	Contractor and specialist skills available	Lump sum approach, means innovation may not be encouraged	Detail design and construction stages
Management type*	Contractor and specialist skills available	None, if contractor can be engaged early	Scheme design and construction stages
Partnering	• Repetition and development • Early involvement of partners	Limited to advice from partners only	All stages
Alliancing	Close relations developed, gain share	• Hidden agendas and vested interests of parties • Often single project	All stages

*More information on these methods can be found in CIRIA SP113, *Planning to build?* (1995). (See 4.3).

Table 3.1 Procurement methods

3.2.2 Feasibility

Part 1(a) Purpose

The feasibility stage explores the options able to meet the client's needs and objectives. It includes choice of the preferred solution, ensuring that it is functionally, technically and financially feasible.

Part 1(b) Planning faster construction on site

Strategic programme

A strategic programme should be established that clearly highlights the targets and phases to completion.

Value management

A structured approach to the evaluation should be adopted from first principles of all the key design, scope, procurement, operational, risk, quality and methodology assumptions. This will enhance the client's need and objectives and ensure that the mix of options is optimised in accordance with the predetermined value criteria. The assessment confirms the appropriateness of faster construction on site and highlights the associated benefits and risks. It also ensures that the project team and client are fully aware of the entire scheme.

Risk management

Risk management procedures should be set up for use throughout the project process. To assist in the selection of options, risks should be identified and assessed. It is important to address high-risk activities that are on the critical path of the programme. Reduce their influence by splitting activities or running them in parallel with other activities.

Environmental and sustainability issues

Recognise the environmental and sustainability issues inherent in faster construction on site. It will probably be necessary to expend equal or more energy over a shorter period to achieve the same end-product earlier. The procedures should ensure that the materials used are sustainable.

Health and safety issues

Implementation of the Construction (Design and Management) Regulations 1994 (CDM) has focused and heightened awareness that health and safety on site demands equal design consideration with other construction requirements. Attempts to increase output to speed construction on site bring with it the imperative demand to maintain safety during construction.

Construction methods and materials

The considerations at this stage will have determined the requirement for selection of the options for methods and materials to achieve the required construction time on site.

INTRODUCTION

PROCUREMENT

FEASIBILITY

CONCEPT

SCHEME

DETAIL

CONSTRUCTION

Part 2 Project option selection

Applying the proposed selection process **(see 2.2)** during the feasibility stage means the following:

ACTIVITY	STEP	EXPLANATION
Identify key issues	**Identify context**	The principal drivers for this stage are the business need, the location, the outputs required from the facility, its expected lifespan, the method of financing the project, the budget and the timescale.
	Identify issues	Business needs drive the issues for faster construction on site. These include business constraints (eg the need to have a factory in operation by the end of September to meet Christmas demand); the client's definition of the facility's functionality; external constraints influencing project development (planning approval, environmental impact); and the facility's intended total life cycle.
List boundaries and assumptions	**List constraints/ opportunities**	Compile the likely project programme, at least in terms of start and finish dates. Think about the effect of location and site on the potential for faster construction. Note all the constraints derived from the funding route (such as a need to use up the budget by a certain date, or the existence of an annual ceiling on funding).
	List assumptions	The underlying assumptions at this stage come under the headings of life and performance, usage, planning approval and environmental integration, and apply to the project as a whole.
Assess and choose preferred option	**Assess and select options**	Various options for the construction solution are put forward and at this stage are broad-brush solutions. In each case they explain the proposed building or structural form, the capacity of the proposed solution (height, footprint, span etc), the cost of ownership (capital and whole-life), overall timescale and budget.
	Evaluate options	Each option is evaluated by balancing risk and value, using criteria such as the degree of functionality achieved, the degree of innovation, level of standardisation, embodied energy and whole-life cost. This will produce a priority order of options.
	Choose preferred option	From the prioritised options, one is chosen. At this stage, criteria include adherence to identified business drivers (business constraints, functionality and external constraints).
Implement chosen option	**Progress to solution**	The selected option should be developed for further analysis. This will consider additional issues, such as the start and completion dates, and whether the project needs to be phased. The aim is to make appropriate decisions to allow the project to move to concept design.

Part 3 Selection of construction methods and materials

Selection of construction methods

Decide which are the critical issues for construction methods at this stage that enable project options to be compared. Review methods at a broad level and evaluate several solutions. Consider the key factors that determine the selection of methods to achieve faster construction on site (**see 2.3.2**):

- context – location, climate, access
- what methods are available for use?
- what are key requirements for safety, environment, sustainability, start and finish dates?

Selection of construction materials

Decide which are the critical issues for construction materials at this stage that enable project options to be compared. Review materials at a broad level and evaluate several solutions. Consider the key factors that determine the selection of materials to enable faster construction on site (**see 2.3.3**):

- context – location, climate, access
- the materials available for use
- the key requirements for safety, durability, cost, appearance, strength, stiffness, sustainability, innovation etc
- consider whether innovative materials are to be used and, if so, their track record
- likely timespan for any materials development.

Part 4 Feasibility stage summary

Aim

Record the basis of the development undertaken by the end of the feasibility stage. It should include the following main headings, which form the basis for development of the design in the concept design stage.

Contents

Client objectives
State the client objectives and identify the actions necessary to achieve those objectives. Identify the owner responsible for the implementation of each action.

Project scope
State the scope of the project, including a description of the extent of the intended build. This should contain a description of the design and construction processes to be adopted and how they will integrate with procurement.

Project master programme
Present the master programme, which confirms the start and finish dates of planning, design and construction, and identifies links to procurement. Set out phasing of the work with basic interfaces, links and dependencies. Identify the critical activities and the critical path of the programme.

Project options
Report on risk management and value management for the options. Identify those activities that are on the critical path and have been considered as options for an accelerated programme. Identify the options for faster construction that were considered when preparing the programme. Report on the chosen faster construction procedures and the reasons for choosing these from the available options. Also record any options not selected, with reasons, to avoid late reviews of the programme.

Methods and materials
Report on the measures to achieve faster construction and outline the methods and materials that may be considered. Include reference to environmental and sustainability issues.

Example

Beazer Partnership Homes is looking at ways of improving the efficiency of the construction process by using factory-made timber frames. Under its Amphion scheme, Beazer aims to have 60 per cent of house components prefabricated in factory conditions, compared to the 15 per cent for a conventional timber development. By shifting house-building from the site to the factory, entire timber-framed walls can be prefabricated, which speeds construction on site and reduces material wastage (**see 4.1.5**).

Example

Small-panel timber construction was used at Cardington.

The components are typically 3.6 m x 2.4 m maximum and can be man-handled, comprising wall panels with door and window openings. They may necessitate a small increase in the number of joints required, but can still be erected faster than masonry construction. Floor joists arrive pre-cut and labelled, but not pre-jointed into floor panels (**see 4.1.5**).

3.3   Design-led stages

3.3.1   Concept design

Part 1(a)   Purpose

The concept design stage develops the preferred solution in terms of architecture, structural form, engineering and internal design. The project team studies options for the major physical and engineering systems and names its preferred solutions. Initial consideration should be given to the manufacture and methods of construction that can meet the desired timetable for completion, together with the materials to be used.

Part 1(b)   Planning faster construction on site

Project programme

The project programme is developed to identify the design, procurement and construction approaches that are proposed for meeting the target dates outlined in the feasibility project programme. Having identified the requirement for faster construction on site, programme durations should be checked to ensure that items can be delivered within the allotted time.

Example

Steel tube piles are used to support masts for overhead cables above railway tracks.

GTBBjv has designed a purpose-made train that includes a piling rig and mast erection unit. A hydraulic piling hammer mounted on an excavator base on the train is used for driving the steel piles. The work takes place in four-hour night possessions.

This method saves time over the conventional method of mast erection. In the UK the mast base is usually of mass concrete with holding-down bolts for the steel mast. Erection is a two-stage operation because of the need to wait for the concrete to set before the mast can be erected (**see 4.1.3**).

Value management

The broad assessment carried out at the feasibility stage is now refined. All the appropriate options should be reviewed to determine whether alternatives might provide better value for money. The value management session carried out at this stage includes all project team members to help establish a clear set of project objectives and full team consensus on the way ahead.

Risk management

Risk assessments allow the relative risk of the options proposed for the project systems to be evaluated. Consider the risks associated with proposed location, height and mass. Assess the proposed faster construction programme in terms of the site's location, access and supporting infrastructure. Decisions about the choice of leading-edge innovative design and construction over traditional methods and materials depend on the nature of the project.

Environmental and sustainability issues
Studies into environmental and sustainability issues need to be undertaken to identify the critical areas of concern arising from the feasibility considerations.

Construction methods and materials

It is important to ensure that the chosen designs are actually going to lead to faster construction. The concept stage starts to develop the form, style and function of the project. Appraisal of the relative merits of the various options should take into account the availability of methods as well as of expertise, infrastructure and transportation. For example, the team should check whether fabricating components off site will speed delivery and installation. Consider availability when choosing materials – for example, whether the source is local to the site or 1000 miles away. Consider what is actually required and whether it can be fabricated and installed faster within the cost and quality constraints.

Example

Tilt-up construction involves site-casting the concrete walls of a building on its floor slab or a separate casting bed and then tilting and lifting them into position by crane. The result is rapid construction using a well-planned process akin to a factory production line but retaining the flexibility of in-situ concrete work. Tilt-up is widely used for one- and two-storey buildings in New Zealand, Australia and particularly the USA. The technique is becoming increasingly popular for buildings of three to five storeys (**see 4.1.5**).

© British Cement Association

Example

Known contamination on part of a brownfield site affected the choice of construction method.

One building proposal required excavation for the foundations to be through the contaminated layer, whereas another, with a shallower foundation, did not necessitate removal of the contaminants. A third solution was to relocate the project away from the contaminant, thus avoiding the problem altogether. An alternative way forward was to remove the contamination in an earlier phase, which would allow a free choice of options. Early removal would avoid delay to the construction, remove constraints on the design and free the site for future development of other phases. Allowing the contamination to remain in place under the building foundations would seal in the pollution and reduce the risk of liberation; it would also avoid further pollution in the area of the tip.

In this example, careful consideration of the options suggested that the choice most sympathetic to faster construction to meet the client's needs was to drive precast concrete piles through the contamination (**see 4.1.3**).

Part 2 Project systems selection

Applying the proposed selection process (see 2.2) during the concept design stage means the following:

ACTIVITY	STEP	EXPLANATION
Identify key issues	**Identify context**	The principal drivers at this stage are the development of an outline specification for the initial planning application and confirmation of the project funding arrangements. This requires the conceptual model for the structure or building to be mostly complete, including the sizing, layout and positioning.
	Identify issues	The issues for faster construction on site derive from the construction methods and materials to be used. Consider whether the level of technology is appropriate for the project. If the need for faster construction is implicit in the project objectives, decide what improvements are necessary.
List boundaries and assumptions	**List constraints/ opportunities**	Consider the impact of the site (greenfield/brownfield/redevelopment/ refurbishment, geology, topography, locality, and size relative to the building or structure) on the intended construction. Anticipate the features that are likely to find favour with the planning authorities (in terms of size, appearance and impact on the neighbourhood).
	List assumptions	Examine the underlying assumptions driving faster construction considerations. Consider the layout and function of the structure or building, and the local infrastructure's ability to support the results of applying faster construction principles.
Assess and choose preferred option	**Assess and select options**	This stage considers project-wide attributes of different construction solutions: site access, site layout, grid/plan/height, availability of materials and workforce.
	Evaluate options	Evaluate each option for its contribution to faster construction by assessing its performance in terms of value and risk. The following criteria should be used: compatibility with the prevailing or projected commercial climate; use of locally available or locally known construction processes and materials; and ability to achieve the construction time required by the feasibility study.
	Choose preferred option	Select a preferred choice from the options evaluated, perhaps with an alternative that can be put forward if planning consent seems likely to be turned down.
Implement chosen option	**Progress to solution**	Develop the chosen option further for "whole project options" by considering the implications for choice of construction methods and materials more closely.

INTRODUCTION
PROCUREMENT
FEASIBILITY
CONCEPT
SCHEME
DETAIL
CONSTRUCTION

INTRODUCTION PROCUREMENT FEASIBILITY CONCEPT SCHEME DETAIL CONSTRUCTION

Part 3 Selection of construction methods and materials

Selection of construction methods

Decide which are the critical issues for construction methods at this stage that enable system options to be compared. Review methods at system level and evaluate several options. Consider the key factors that determine the selection of methods to achieve faster construction on site (**see 2.3.2**).

Site location
The location of the structure on the chosen site is often fundamental to the success of the faster construction initiative. Attention should be paid to site topography, especially noting potential sources of problems such as the water table, contamination, existing structures, substations and overhead high-load cables.

Orientation
The orientation of the project could dramatically affect the speed of construction. A project located some distance from the site access is likely to have more space available for off-loading facilities and storage. If the project structure is close to the access point, or obstructs or restricts access to the remainder of the site, then faster construction is likely to be more difficult.

Configuration
The mass, height or plan shape of a project will significantly affect the ease and speed of construction. While massed elements may speed construction, they may also obstruct the site and so slow progress. For example, large ductwork elements reduce the number of joint connections that need to be made and so reduce construction time. However, the greater size and length of the elements might hinder access and slow the process down.

Prefabrication, pre-assembly and modularisation
Consider the potential of methods based on prefabrication, pre-assembly and modularisation (**see 4.2**).

Selection of construction materials

Decide which are the critical issues for construction materials that enable system options to be compared. Review materials at system level and evaluate several options. Consider the key factors that determine the selection of materials to achieve faster construction on site (**see 2.3.3**):

- client opinions
- site and environment issues
- safety
- preliminary CDM assessment
- the properties (eg strength, stiffness, compatibility, embodied energy) required
- durability – the design life required
- cost – amount, upper limit
- appearance – the method of specifying this
- appropriate standards
- operating/whole-life costs
- approvals.

Newer materials such as high-strength concrete may promote faster construction times, but should be adopted only if all on the construction team are committed to understanding and facilitating their correct use. Use of new materials requires greater effort in design, planning and construction technique if the potential for faster construction on site is to be realised. Initiate any trials that may be required.

Part 4 Concept design summary

Aim

Record the basis of the development undertaken in the concept design stage under the following main headings. They form the basis for developing the design in the scheme design stage.

Contents

Project master programme
The project master programme embraces all aspects of the project. It includes statutory authority approval, utilities planning, legal matters, rights of light and over-sailing. It also covers all design activity and an outline of construction and commissioning.

Outline procurement strategy
Identify the procurement strategy using the principles set out in the procurement section. After assessing the requirements of the project and the relationship between design and construction, report the procurement route. The outline construction programme delineates the overall construction period as well as phasing. There may be benefits in separating identifiable packages of work, such as demolition or piling, into phases.

Buildability studies
Few single processes will bring greater project benefit than the skilful review of buildability. Careful sequencing of activities can considerably shorten construction time on site.

Building systems review
This is the time to review the global systems proposed for the project. The review should cover the building's appearance and whether it should be one large structure or two small ones. Other points to consider are whether the installation should have natural or mechanical ventilation. Statements of the requirements upon the systems should be made, in readiness for scheme design.

Update of risk reviews
Risk reviews will be updates of the feasibility stage assessments in the light of the developed design at concept stage. New subjects will be included in the assessments that arise due to development of the design. The concept report appraises and reports on the outcome of these assessments. For example, site conditions may be re-appraised in the knowledge of further design, while procurement may be assessed for the first time. Risk reviews are brought together formally in the project risk register.

Construction methods and materials
At close of the concept stage, the report should identify the perceived way forward using the materials considered appropriate for the project. For example, cladding may need to be effective for 25 years and services for 12 years. Proposals for addressing environmental and sustainability issues should be included.

3.3.2 Scheme design

Part 1(a) Purpose

At the scheme design stage, the general arrangements are developed and co-ordinated design takes place, fixing the major design systems and elements. Co-ordination is essential to ensure accurate predictions can be made about cost, safety, quality, environmental, sustainability and operational performance. Planning of the manufacture and construction methods takes place, together with integration of the appropriate materials and products for achieving faster construction on site.

Part 1(b) Planning faster construction on site

Project programme

The project programme is developed at the scheme stage to demonstrate the way project elements will be built. The systems are identified, scheduled and sequenced. Confirmation of the systems enables programme logic dependencies to be shown in some detail. At this stage, the programme sets out the design and installation of elements, but not the detailed connections and interfaces.

Value engineering

It is important for the project team to assess the financial value of individual building elements and components. It may be useful to undertake whole-life cost assessments of options. All appropriate options are considered in a formal workshop environment and the impact of any potential change is reviewed against the brief's risk, programme, procurement, quality, cost and methodology aspects. The main criterion is to eliminate waste and over-specification, to ensure that construction meets the project targets at lowest cost.

Risk management

Assessment of system types dominates work for the scheme design. Risk management offers a testing regime that ensures the right system is chosen and that identifies risk levels associated with that choice. For example, risk management techniques can compare the merits and risks of a services system that heats and ventilates with only ducted air through variable air volume units with one that is supplemented with fan coil units. The risk register is a dynamic document and is developed into a detailed risk statement for the project.

Identified need for faster construction on site

The need for faster construction significantly affects, or is affected by, the scheme designs. These latter are chosen not only on their own construction activity speed and duration, but also by the collective effect of the associated activities in the scheme design.

Environmental and sustainability issues

The proposals for addressing environmental and sustainability issues are examined in detail and definitive solutions are developed in conjunction with other design parameters.

INTRODUCTION

PROCUREMENT

FEASIBILITY

CONCEPT

SCHEME

DETAIL

CONSTRUCTION

Part 2 Project element selection

Apply the proposed selection process (**see 2.2**) during scheme design stage means the following:

ACTIVITY	STEP	EXPLANATION
Identify key issues	**Identify context**	The principal driver for this stage is the establishment of the major systems of the development. The outcome of the outline planning application may impose further constraints on the project.
	Identify issues	The issues for faster construction come from the consideration of individual systems within the building or structure, in particular, understanding the interactions between adjacent areas of work.
List boundaries and assumptions	**List constraints/ opportunities**	Determine the opportunities that exist for parallel working on multiple workfaces or for using large-scale prefabrication. Decide how the sequence of works can be arranged to improve construction times, or reduce the risk of delays. List the parts of the building or structure that are on the critical path.
	List assumptions	Assume that planning constraints can be overcome while keeping within the project objectives. Assume that the techniques for construction are valid in terms of material and labour availability.
Assess and choose preferred option	**Assess and select options**	For faster construction, the options should identify where it is possible to use mass production, off-site fabrication and standard elements. Pay special attention to systems that have long lead times (eg lifts, prefabricated cladding) and to elements that can be sourced from only one or two suppliers (eg particular stone finishes). Consider how the interfaces between systems are expected to work.
	Evaluate options	Each of the alternatives for the systems can now be evaluated in terms of the risks against achieving faster construction. These will include reassessment against national and local economic conditions, availability of suppliers of plant, labour, materials, components, design co-ordination and construction interfaces.
	Choose preferred option	Selection of the option for detailed development requires compliance with the main criteria. These include the project programme, requirement for on-site labour, the extent to which local infrastructure and location of suppliers is compatible with off-site fabrication, and the capacity of the site for plant storage and bulk deliveries.
Implement chosen option	**Progress to solution**	Time spent preparing proper information and considering all the detailed issues before construction can be more than made up through improvements in the speed of construction on site. Benefits also accrue through improving health and safety standards and minimising delays or stoppages due to accidents resulting from unsafe working practices.

Part 3 Selection of construction methods and materials

Selection of construction methods

Decide which are the critical issues for construction methods at this stage that enable element options to be compared. Review methods at an element level and evaluate several options. Consider the factors that determine the selection of methods for achieving faster construction on site (**see 2.3.2**).

Grid
The size of the building grid affects both the proposed elements within the project and the choice of construction method. Larger elements bring economies because fewer elements have to be installed, but they may be harder to handle.

Systems
It is not always easy to compare different systems directly. For example, a steelwork structure might be quicker to erect than concrete but require painting and fire protection, whereas concrete will not. A lightning protection system bonded to reinforcement in concrete could provide economies of time, but the risk of continuity test failure might necessitate installing tapes as well.

Example
Thurrock Lakeside Car Parks

The choice of a hybrid reinforced concrete frame using in-situ beams, prefabricated hollow-core floor slabs and precast concrete stairs proved vital to meet the faster construction programme without any sacrifice of quality and economy. Off-site factory production enabled stringent control of all the precast units produced off the critical path. Extensive mechanisation and standardised, simplified site work were also critical to faster construction. All reinforcement cages were prefabricated away from the workface. Precast floor planks provided a safe working platform for subsequent activities. Pumped concrete with high early strengths was also used (**see 4.1.4**).

Layout
Generally, standardising the layout generates economies of time, because it allows repetition of elements. If all units or elements are the same and in the same location relative to the grid and levels, time savings can be made. There is no need to find bespoke units on site, and installation is simplified because elements are all fixed in the same way, avoiding an additional learning process.

Material combinations and products
Initially it might appear that using one material throughout makes for faster construction. However, this may not always be the case. There might be time constraints affecting a single material system that can be avoided by subtly modifying material combinations (**see 4.2**).

Selection of construction materials

Decide which are the critical issues for construction materials at this stage that enable element options to be compared. Review materials at an element level and evaluate several options. Consider the factors that determine the selection of materials for achieving faster construction on site (**see 2.3.3**).

From starting with a broad combination of materials, scheme design should develop firm ideas about components and the degree of off-site fabrication.

Select best options on the basis of:

- balanced comparison of factors
- awareness of adjacent materials
- cost
- buildability
- supply
- delivery
- storage of products.

Part 4 Scheme design summary

Aim

Record the basis of the development undertaken in the scheme design stage. It could include the following main headings, which are used for design development in the detailed production design.

Contents

Project master programme

The project master programme shows the way the job is to be built. It identifies the chosen systems. The decision may be cut-and-fill for earthworks, a chilled ceiling for services cooling, composite floors, and acer trees and a lake for landscaping.

Procurement programme

The scheme design will have contributed to the information required for tendering or negotiating the contract for construction. The scheme design stage is when the big choices between the faster construction options are made.

Construction programme

The opportunities for faster construction on site are incorporated into the programme. The designers make their major decisions and the construction plan interprets the design in terms of faster construction on site. Careful design assessments promote the development of a fast programme for construction. A good construction programme will have:

- activities with few dependencies on critical path
- activities with few supporting links on critical path
- low-risk items on critical path.

Example

Corrosion protection often represents a production bottleneck in the fabrication process. Preparation and application of coatings are relatively slow processes, yet their performance is critical to long-term durability.

It is important to limit the amount of reworking and making good. Different approaches to corrosion protection produce vastly different results; blast-cleaning and painting before fabrication may be expected to lead to far more rework than fabrication of whole sections prior to blasting and painting.

Construction time and cost can also be reduced by moving away from multi-coat paint specifications and looking at the total applied costs associated with superior products such as high-solids-compliant coatings and the latest generation of glass flake materials and polysiloxanes. Although such materials are often more expensive per tin, it is possible to get the steel in and out of the paint shop and on truck to site within 24 hours.

It is worth looking carefully at the specification for corrosion protection. Unless protection is essential, it should not be used. Similarly, if the final appearance is not important, then do not use the finishes. If corrosion protection is required, use specifications that make the fabricators' life easy and avoid site painting **(see 4.1.5)**.

Construction method statement

At this stage, the buildability studies will have led to a scheme design that meets the faster construction criteria. Activities, both individual and collective, should be able to be carried out quickly. The report defines the milestones for the scheme design. Buildability studies confirm that the scheme design is efficient and economical for faster construction on site.

Detail design programme

The detail design programme sets out the plan for the detail design of the next phase. The programme shows the way the design for faster construction is expanded to the greatest level of design detail. The detailed programme delineates the resourcing of the detail design and the design deliverables that are to be issued to allow procurement and construction on site to proceed.

Risk management

The risk register emerges from the risk management process and addresses such project issues as the impact of faster construction on site, health and safety risks, environmental aspects and sustainability issues.

Example

At the Inland Revenue building in Nottingham, standardised precast concrete units and prefabricated brick cladding were used. Bricklayers and concretors worked in a favourable, indoor environment where excellent tolerances were achieved in a fast construction time **(see 4.1.4)**.

3.3.3 Detailed production design

Part 1(a) Purpose

The detail production design stage sees the preparation of production information. Consultants, suppliers and contractors detail all the project's components and finalise plans for the manufacture and assembly operations, including details of the materials to be used.

Part 1(b) Planning faster construction on site

Project programme

The project programme incorporates the information necessary for the detail design for faster construction on site. Programmes include activities for design and scheduling of elements and connections. For example, it might look at the intended sequence for construction of a propped retaining wall. It considers whether this allows the builder to progress in a fast, economical and logical manner, or if it leaves the builder tied up during temporary works until the permanent structure is complete and the propping action is functioning.

Value engineering

There is only limited scope for value-engineering the design at this late stage. Programme delays due to redesign, extra fees etc may offset the advantage of potential cost or value efficiencies. At this stage, value engineering is likely to be component-orientated and involve input from the supply chain, thereby increasing risk from procurement and cost certainty perspectives.

Risk management

During detail design, risk assessments assess the "nuts and bolts" of the design to ensure that details can be fabricated and assembled, either in the factory or on site, within the time constraints. For example, it might consider whether the design decision to use hardwood timber prefabricated door sets presents the least risk to the programme. It might look at the advantages of using site controls to manage the process of early subframes, against the use of traditional hardwood doors and frames.

Component detailing

The designer should create details that allow the scheme design to be built quickly. Detail design will produce information in successive levels of detail. Scheme layout sections and elevations are upgraded as more details are added. Details, sections and plans now show the design of all the project details required.

INTRODUCTION PROCUREMENT FEASIBILITY CONCEPT SCHEME DETAIL CONSTRUCTION

INTRODUCTION
PROCUREMENT
FEASIBILITY
CONCEPT
SCHEME
DETAIL
CONSTRUCTION

Part 2 Project component selection

Applying the proposed selection process (see 2.2) during detailed production design means the following:

ACTIVITY	STEP	EXPLANATION
Identify key issues	Identify context	The principal drivers for this stage of design are the chosen scheme for the project, including the selected major systems. The overall objectives for faster construction drive the development of details that can be fabricated and installed or constructed within the desired time envelope.
	Identify issues	The issues for faster construction at this stage include buildability and assembly of components, delivery schedules for materials and components, detailed health and safety implications of the design for the constructor, and detailed programming of activities.
List boundaries and assumptions	List constraints/ opportunities	Constraints include the limitations of the range of standard components, the physical capacity of the site and its infrastructure (craneage, welfare facilities etc) to allow a large workforce or work in several areas at once. Opportunities for faster construction include repetition in fabrication or installation of components, while still adhering to the design intent. Ideally, repetition of both fabrication and installation offer the best opportunities for faster construction on site.
	List assumptions	An underlying assumption at this stage is that time spent on detailed design and planning will be more than compensated for by a shorter period actually on site. There is also a presumption of use of standard components, of off-site fabrication and assembly (to improve on-site productivity), and for long-lead time items to be activated in advance.
Assess and choose preferred option	Assess and select options	A range of options for the detailed design of particular elements should be considered. Preference should be given to off-the-shelf items, or to elements that can be assembled away from the workface (whether this is actually on- or off-site). Construction details should be standardised to minimise the risk of confusion and delay on site. Use should be made of emerging or new technologies that can accelerate the construction phase (within the confines of quality assurance).
	Evaluate options	Each option for the construction elements should be evaluated in terms of achievement of the faster construction objectives. This may also include assessment of buildability, minimising the number of discrete site activities and minimising the number of interfaces between adjacent trades.
	Choose preferred option	Choose the option for each component which best meets the criteria set at this stage for arrangements that can be fabricated and installed or constructed to meet the programme requirements.
Implement chosen option	Progress to solution	Development of the detailed design requires close co-ordination between all project team members (designers, suppliers and constructors) and preparation of trial panels, mock-ups or pre-assemblies to verify construction and installation details. The pre-construction health and safety plan should also be completed, to provide the relevant information to the construction team.

Part 3 Selection of construction methods and materials

Selection of construction methods

Decide which are the critical issues for construction methods at this stage that enable component options to be compared. Review methods at a component level and evaluate several options. Consider the key factors determining the selection of methods that achieve faster construction on site (see 2.3.2).

Repetition

Repetition is a most effective way to speed up activities. This can involve the use of standardised components installed in the same way each time. For detail installation, "repetition" might mean standardising the grade of concrete everywhere on the project at 35 N/mm^2, avoiding the additional management time of checking on each pour. Repetition might involve keeping an element to a constant dimension or position – eg all lighting pendants are in the centre of every room, or extract vents are always 150 mm down from the ceiling.

Standard modules

Use of identical or standard modules speeds construction because it simplifies the checking of drawings, fabrication and installation. The principle can be applied by using a standard dense concrete block for all blockwork, or by employing standard air handling units in roof plant or standard toilet pods within the building.

Avoid bespoke details

Bespoke details tend to slow the installation process. One-off elements are time-consuming, from detailing at the design stage and developing prototype systems through fabrication, and up to installation, with its associated learning curve for a new element.

Tolerances

To facilitate faster construction, it is prudent wherever possible to increase tolerances for the faster installation within the specified requirements. This need not result in an inferior job.

Selection of construction materials

Decide which are the critical issues for construction materials at this stage that enable component options to be compared. Review materials at a component level and evaluate several solutions. Consider the key factors determining materials selection to achieve faster construction on site. Develop detailed specifications for materials and design to be right first time with active involvement of all in the supply chain (see 2.3.3).

Consider how different operations should be programmed and decide whether the sequence is appropriate. Determine on the critical steps. Set out the ways in which materials should be selected to achieve faster construction times. Ascertain which materials contribute to predictable construction times and which might cause delays due to the effects of climate, application, drying out/curing time etc (see 4.2).

- Consider the extent to which prefabrication can be used to reduce the risk of delays due to materials.

- Identify critical success factors, targets and deliverables.

- Determine appropriate tests for monitoring progress and ensuring achievement of targets.

- Issue specification with the agreement of all in the supply chain.

- Represent the materials selected on a modified chart for the records.

Example

Lighting column foundations, M25 Junctions 8 to 10

The original contract documents called for a bored pile for every lighting column. As part of the value engineering exercises during the design-and-build contract, and in consultation with the Highways Agency staff who had developed and tested the safety barrier design, the lighting column foundations were incorporated within the central reserve concrete barriers. This reduced the construction time of the programme's critical sequential activities, resulting in significant cost savings and ensuring the correct deformation performance of the barriers (see 4.1.3).

Example

A pontoon mooring is secured by guide piles grouped in threes for each mooring structure. The vertical tolerance for the guide pile must be exact, to allow the mooring collar to rise and fall with the tide. However, the other two piles in the group are simply structural supports for the mooring structure cap and require no such accuracy. By taking this into account, the contractor can carry out the piling of the non-guide piles from a piling barge at a greater rate, reducing overall construction time (see 4.1.3).

INTRODUCTION

PROCUREMENT

FEASIBILITY

CONCEPT

SCHEME

DETAIL

CONSTRUCTION

CONSTRUCTION   DETAIL   SCHEME   CONCEPT   FEASIBILITY   PROCUREMENT   INTRODUCTION

Part 4 Detailed production design summary

Aim

Record the basis of the development undertaken in the detailed production design stage. It should include the following main headings, which form the basis of development of the construction site assembly and installation stage.

Contents

Detail construction programme
The construction programme indicates in detail the activities for construction. The design for faster construction on site presents the contractor with a platform for developing the planning for construction.

Outline commissioning programme
Faster construction should allow the rapid process to continue through commissioning to ensure timely operation of the project. These programmes of work are reported here, outlining the chosen programme procedures and the parties responsible for implementation of commissioning.

Outline operation and maintenance plan
Knowing the design and commissioning procedures, the outline procedures for operation and maintenance can be reported. The initial report should demonstrate that designing and constructing for early completion has not prejudiced good design and has not complicated or increased the building's whole-life maintenance requirements.

Outline demolition strategy
This report describes the procedures identified during the design for the safe and fast demolition strategy. Faster and safer demolition is an important part of the construction process. Facilities for demolition may be incorporated into the design and construction. For example, the strategy might describe procedures for removing a cable-stayed steelwork exhibition building or for the demolition and dismantling of a load-bearing brickwork building.

Buildability reviews
Buildability reviews at detail design stage provide the last design opportunity to check buildability before construction. Being at the end of the design process, they are likely to have the least impact on the outcome of further construction.

Risk management
The risk register is completed and made available as a briefing document for the construction team.

Information for the health and safety plan
The planning supervisor will collate information from the team for the health and safety plan. The information relates to design assumptions and risks for faster construction, and outlines safe procedures necessary to achieve the programme.

3.4 Construction-led stage

3.4.1 Construction site assembly and installation

Part 1(a) Purpose

The construction stage sees the implementation of the plans for manufacture, assembly and on-site construction. Work is carried out in accordance with the relevant plans and programmes set during the design and procurement processes.

Part 1(b) Planning faster construction on site

Project programme

The project programme in the construction phase will develop construction planning of activities on site. Into the overall project programme will be incorporated packages of work contributing to faster construction. Work will be packaged to optimise on time and work faces. A balance of speed and overlapping disciplines will be tempered with avoiding too many trades in an area, thus reducing output and efficiency as well as compromising safety.

Value engineering

Value engineering at the construction stage only succeeds if carried out with the full knowledge and agreement of the contractor as well as the design team. It is important to consider the implications of change at this stage, along with changes in risk allocation, programme implementation, maintainability, operational costs and the value of the finished product. Value engineering at this stage is likely to relate to component specifications, construction methodology and alternative suppliers. Benefits for faster construction or cost efficiencies are likely to be small.

Risk management

Risk management in the construction phase takes place within several constraints. The design phase provided a faster construction opportunity. Risk assessments review the construction options of the detailed design. Procurement has been organised and prefabrication optimised. The construction risk assessments test all these for the last time before site installation. The construction options are limited now to some improvements to, and implementation of, the intended design.

Construction programme

The construction programme, with input by the specialist contractor and suppliers, will have been developed with the co-operation and participation of the entire design team. The contractor has prepared the programme after checking with suppliers for performance and delivery periods. Close liaison has taken place with package subcontractors to ensure they have sufficient production capabilities. The client team may already have ordered some long lead-in items and the contractor is monitoring early order progress.

Example

Many universities and institutes are researching self-compacting concrete. The Kajima Corporation has used the material in more than 50 projects in Japan since 1990. It offers the potential for faster construction and cost savings by:

- reduced reliance on the operative to vibrate the concrete
- self-levelling, which allows placement through smaller openings and more innovative construction methods
- lack of segregation, which permits increased pour depths, allowing greater volumes of concrete to be placed in each pour.

Example

Panablock, produced by Marshall's Building Products, can be used for rapid creation of pre-formed structural walling. It allows rapid construction of a skin that provides a temporary weatherproof finish with a high insulation value. All work on the inside of the building – including occupancy – may thus take place before completion of the external cladding. Panablock has also been used for applications such as scout huts and village halls. A temporary waterproof paint is applied to the external face and the building used for two or three years while funds are raised to pay for the permanent masonry external cladding.

The material has been used for refurbishment work on multi-storey blocks. The building is stripped to the frame and a new insulated cladding applied. The Panablock is cut to match the existing floor height and is rapidly installed, allowing the building to be occupied during attachment of the external cladding.

Example

Rosewood Development, Basingstoke

C50 concrete was used instead of C35 to speed construction. The cement type and specially developed admixtures were used in the concrete mix to facilitate strength gain. Similar techniques are used widely for road construction, repairs and airport runway work (see 4.1.4).

INTRODUCTION

PROCUREMENT

FEASIBILITY

CONCEPT

SCHEME

DETAIL

CONSTRUCTION

Part 2 Project implementation on site selection

Applying the proposed process (**see 2.2**) during this stage means the following:

ACTIVITY	STEP	EXPLANATION
Identify key issues	**Identify context**	The level of detail in the production information provides the context for faster construction at assembly/installation stage. The construction team's understanding of the development of the design to allow faster construction on site also helps define the context at this stage.
	Identify issues	Issues affecting the achievement of faster construction include: approval process for fabrication drawings (including the technology used for communication between team members); adherence to the programme of fabrication, delivery, assembly and installation; appropriate welfare facilities for site workers; health and safety considerations; monitoring procedures for time, cost and quality; communication procedures for approving enhancements to the method statements.
List boundaries and assumptions	**List constraints/ opportunities**	Constraints include the availability of subcontract labour/specialist tradesmen, and weather conditions (particularly conditions more severe than the programme allowed for). Opportunities include micro-replanning of the construction process to improve interfaces and open up parallel workfaces on the site, and use of productivity measures (such as CALIBRE) to identify tasks where productivity can be improved.
	List assumptions	For faster construction during site assembly, the following assumptions should be made: the design intent is not changed, no design variations are made except in response to unforeseen circumstances, workforce continuity and commitment to the project is achieved.
Assess and choose preferred option	**Assess and select options**	Options can be chosen to improve the potential for faster construction. These include: increasing the site labour force, using more or larger items of plant, relaxing the specification for particular works (taking care to assess the knock-on effect on other items of work), increasing the level of risk in the project by using a less well tried (but faster) construction method or an innovative material.
	Evaluate options	The risk and value associated with each option should be evaluated and compared so as to reach the most beneficial solution within the constraints of the project.
	Choose preferred option	Choose an option that creates the least disruption to the remainder of the construction programme.
Implement chosen option	**Progress to solution**	The development of the solution for faster construction at site assembly and installation stage requires assessment of the likely learning curve for innovative methods or materials. For this, the time benefit should be weighed against changes in cost, health and safety, quality and availability of skills.

Part 3 Selection of construction methods and materials

Selection of construction methods

Decide which are the critical issues for construction methods in the specific circumstances at this stage that will enable construction options to be compared. Review the methods at a detailed level and evaluate several options. Consider the key factors that determine methods of selection that lead to faster construction on site (**see 2.3.2**).

Implement agreed methods
The agreed methods outlined in the scheme design and further developed in detail design are incorporated into the contractor's method statements. These methods are now ready to implement on the site. Method statements should be updated as often as necessary to take account of:

- developing design details
- refinement of construction methods
- changing conditions.

Method statements cover temporary works as well as the permanently installed works. Faster construction is as reliant on well-designed temporary works as it is on permanent ones.

Example
A building can be generally piled for pile foundations at ground level. However, in this example, the lift and stair core are founded below floor level. The lift core was piled at the same time from ground level with blind-bored piling for the lift and stair core pile-cap. (Blind boring means that there is no reinforcement or concrete in the top part of the shaft.) This allowed one early visit of the piling rig and avoided the need for a return visit when the stair and lift core area was excavated. It also avoided isolating the site with access ramps for positioning the piling rig into the lower excavation (**see 4.1.3**).

Installation tolerances
The design team has given the contractor every opportunity to fabricate and install faster. In turn, the contractor wants to take advantage of generous tolerances during installation. This need not mean that the client receives an inferior product. A careful balance has to be maintained. The situation is similar to design specification. Clients and designers should be willing to specify the maximum tolerance consistent with achieving the desired product. There is little point in insisting on a particular surface line and level of finish simply because that is the finish specified elsewhere, if in this instance the finish is out of sight. However, it is important to strike a balance, because a proliferation of variations might make checking so complex that it negates the benefits.

Selection of construction materials

Decide which are the critical issues for construction materials in the specific circumstances at this stage that will enable construction options to be compared. Review materials at a detailed level and evaluate several options. Consider the key factors determining the selection of materials that lead to faster construction on site (**see 2.4.3**).

Materials should perform in terms of:

- properties
- supply
- storage
- ease of installation/assembly/trial erection
- appearance.

Testing should facilitate faster construction on site, allowing detection and resolution of defects at the earliest opportunity, with a target of zero defects. Accept changes that do not compromise the original intent agreed by the whole project team, but guard against materials being substituted unknowingly. Retain informed selection procedures to ensure zero defects in the long term.

INTRODUCTION PROCUREMENT FEASIBILITY CONCEPT SCHEME DETAIL CONSTRUCTION

Part 4 Construction site assembly and installation summary

Aim

Regularly record the development undertaken in the construction site assembly and installation stage. Include the following main headings to use as the basis for the periodic construction reports.

Contents

Status report

Report on the status of the site assembly or construction, paying special attention to those activities requiring faster construction. The report identifies:

- the issue of design information
- supplier performance
- prefabrication or pre-assembly performance
- site assembly or construction performance.

Forecast to complete

It is possible that the proposals referred to in the status report will not remain on programme. They may proceed faster or more slowly than expected. In that situation, the planned programme will need to be revisited. New forecasts for completion will be prepared for inclusion in a revised programme.

Commissioning report

Commissioning is part of the faster construction process and the client has a considerable interest in the success of this final stage of the process. The report outlines the progress of commissioning and the success of the accelerated plan.

The report demonstrates that the key to the successful commissioning phase lies in:

- clear direction as to the scope of duties for commissioning
- clear direction as to the responsibilities for commissioning
- adequate money allocated for the task
- competent parties selected to carry out the work.

Attention to the detail of the above criteria may in itself be sufficient to promote the faster construction required.

Risk management report

The report may be a document prepared and issued at progress meetings. It covers the status of the risk register and refers to site safety procedures, the health and safety plan and the development of the health and safety file. Health and safety considerations are of great importance during design and implementation of faster construction procedures. Naturally, the main concern is to prevent injury on site. Furthermore, sites that are badly disrupted by incidents suffer lower morale and slower construction rates. In extreme situations, unhelpful design or construction can lead to serious accidents. HSE investigations delay construction further, if they cause stoppages or disruption. A well-prepared and updated risk register maintained throughout the project's life provides an excellent audit trial.

Example

Use of "temperature-matched curing" at Queen Elizabeth Bridge, Dartford, allowed concrete strength to be assessed directly from the structure rather than necessitating waiting for 28-day cube compliance. Formwork removal times were minimised and the overall sequences in the construction programme were achieved with optimum cycle times for concrete pours.

Example

In the refurbishment of No 1 Finsbury Square, London, intumescent paints were sprayed directly on to unprimed/primed surfaces off site. This resulted in improved cost efficiency and reliability, and reduced construction time on site. Damage on site was remedied quickly and easily to ensure faster construction times were successfully achieved **(see 4.1.5)**.

3.5 Examples of achieving faster construction on site through design

Project stage				
Feasibility	**Concept**	**Scheme**	**Detail**	**Construction**
Reorientate the structure				
Reduce the project scope				
Phase the work				
Change the market window for construction				
	Simplify the product being built			
	Simplify the building process			
	Modularise the work			
	Reduce work below ground			
	Reduce work at height			
	Improve site access, horizontal and vertical			
	Use local materials			
	Use local expertise			
	Improve the infrastructure			
		Allow more workfaces in design		
		Reduce potential for defective work		
		Use larger units		
		Use fewer units		
		Employ larger labour resource		
		Employ larger plant resource		
		Employ larger material resource		
			Overlap the activities	
			Increase the lap of activities	
			Change the materials	
			Change the process	
			Standardise elements	
			Prefabricate work off site	
			Organise early enabling works contract	
				Simplify the details
				Standardise the connections
				Increase the gain of strength
				Reduce concrete curing time
				Increase tolerances
				Plan to:
				Introduce parallel working
				Accelerate the activities
				Increase labour
				Increase plant
				Raise production

4.1 Achieving faster construction on site

This section provides information for use in the selection process described in Sections 2 and 3. Construction sequences and activities should be reviewed at each stage of the project, together with the proposed methods and materials. Members of the project team and suppliers need to consider the effect of faster completion upon their contribution to the project (**see 2.1**).

4.1.1 The site

Faster construction on site can be achieved by the following:

Extra space for the site compound. Ensure that the materials storage space is sufficient to supply the site at the speed of anticipated delivery and construction demand (**see CIRIA SP146** *Managing materials and components on site*).

Maintain good horizontal site access. This consists of site roads, conveyors, scaffolds and pumps. Horizontal site access is usually the initial point of entry to the work area, so horizontal site handling capacity should not restrict construction progress.

Maintain good vertical site access. This consists of cranes, hoists, lifts, pumps, ladders and stairs. Vertical handling usually forms the double-handling activity and elevates the materials to the required level of the workface. This leg of the transportation is often the limiting factor for volume of supply for construction progress (**see CIRIA SP121** *Temporary access to the workface*).

Keep the site compound well surfaced, well organised, clean and tidy. This helps minimise damage and soiling of materials, which can then be included into the works immediately, avoiding the delays caused by reordering stocks to replace those damaged (**see CIRIA SP146** *Managing materials and components on site*).

Good messing/drying facilities for labour. Operatives able to rest during work breaks in clean, dry, quiet and warm surroundings can return to the faster construction environment refreshed and able to work safely.

Good access for material/plant deliveries. Comprehensive facilities for transport arrivals and departures ensure a rapid and safe turnaround. Materials may arrive by road, water, railway, pipeline or conveyors. Delivery not only covers transport to the materials storage area, but also onward to the workface.

Delivery of bulk materials in large quantities. The familiar concept of transportation of bulk materials by road may not be appropriate for faster construction on a particular site. Large quantities can be transported by rail (eg reinforcement/steelwork) or barge (eg ballast from a dredger). Large volumes can be transported shorter distances by pipeline (eg water/gas/oil/chalk/cement/concrete) or conveyor (eg excavated material/fill) as these modes can function 24 hours a day, seven days a week.

Care of factory finishes. Reliable protection should be ensured throughout the process to avoid rework, which causes delay, additional cost and usually an inferior product.

Backup plant. For support during peak demand periods when carrying out fast activities, eg mobile cranes supporting tower cranes.

Robust survey station system. A reliable survey system can be used quickly and with confidence to produce accurate and consistent results when setting out and levelling (**see CIRIA SP145** *Setting out procedures*).

Security at boundary, site-gate and secure areas. Security during working hours, at night and weekends avoids delays resulting from vandalism, theft, protests and sit-ins.

Safe site, with well-protected excavations, drops or elevated accesses. Avoids disruption to work while accidents are being attended to or subject to HSE investigations

(see CIRIA R166 *CDM Regulations – work sector guidance for designers;* SP151 *Site safety handbook*).

Effective site lighting system. Allows work to continue during hours of inadequate natural light.

De-watering system that will maintain good working areas and access. Ensure operatives are not working in flooded conditions. Effective de-watering improves the work rate.

Contaminated sites. Decontamination procedures for contaminated sites avoid or mitigate delays (**see CIRIA R132 and SP119** *A guide for safe working on contaminated sites;* SP101–112 *Remedial treatment for contaminated land* (Vols I–XII).

Comprehensive project communication. Lack of understanding by parties involved in the project of project progress adversely affects faster construction. Communication can be by word of mouth at meetings either in groups or individually. Letters, memos and faxes form part of this information network. Other methods include land-line and mobile telephones, radios, email and CCTV. For fast transmission of email etc, an electronic office should be set up to act as the communications hub. Set up a controlled website on the Internet for project communications, including issue of mail, drawings and documents (**see 1.4**).

Liaise with the local community. Aim to answer local queries and objections as soon as possible. Consider setting up a 24-hour help line. Large projects merit the appointment of a community liaison officer.

4.1.2 Demolition/enabling works

Faster construction during demolition and enabling works can be achieved by the following:

Consider whether demolition is necessary. Avoid if possible. Endeavour to carry out the project around the redundant structure, or utilise parts of it. This could be particularly effective where both faster construction and contaminated materials are involved.

Separate enabling works contract and utilities. This will avoid an early enabling works package that might slow the main works. Plan for early diversion of gas, water and electricity by statutory undertakers.

Arisings, demolished or surplus materials removed to tip. If scrap has zero value, the demolition contractor gains no benefit from salvaging materials, so he will not be slowed in selection of material (**see CIRIA Report SP133** *Waste minimisation in construction site guide*; **SP134** *Waste minimisation and recycling in construction – design manual*).

Demolition, use of explosives, CO₂ cartridges. These methods are under-used in the UK but can be effective, fast de-construction tools. Limitations include local authority restrictions on the use of explosives, and inappropriate site environment. Clearing up afterwards might also be a disincentive.

Use of water-cutting/thermic lances. In the appropriate site situation, water-cutting or thermic lances can be effective tools for dismantling constructed elements. These applications have the advantage that they are relatively quiet and fast if used over long activity periods.

Use of diamond drilling/saws. In appropriate site situations diamond drilling and saws are effective tools for dismantling constructed elements. The applications are relatively fast and accurate, and are less noisy than conventional breakers.

Separation of machine operation and labour operatives. Site activities should be planned and programmed to allow the separate zoning of machines and labour. Complete separation and lack of interaction improve safety and the speed of activities.

Use of mobile cruncher/crusher/ compactor on site. The use of this equipment usually requires substantial areas of the site on which to operate. It is ideal for fast de-construction on a disciplined site operating plant-only and labour-only site areas for demolition.

Timing of works with respect to nearby neighbours. Consider relative merits of one relatively short but potentially intense period of de-construction disruption or a longer overall period carried out over, say, weekends (**see CIOB** *Considerate Constructors Scheme*).

Phasing of demolition. Overlap phases of demolition or enabling works with the main construction if site is large enough.

Demolition and removal of contaminated material. This is most effectively scheduled as a separate earlier work package. If carried out at the same time as other packages, all staff might need to vacate the site during certain operations to remove contaminated material (**see CIRIA SP102** *Remedial treatment for contaminated land Vol II – decommissioning, decontamination and demolition*).

Divert high-risk services out of the work area. High-voltage cables, transformers and gas mains relocated away from the construction area allow faster construction activities to proceed unimpeded.

Separate mass works from detail. Separating mass work (eg cut and fill) from detailed works (eg services installation/ diversions) opens the way for the contractor to use plant with more output. In cut-and-fill earthworks, for example, this approach allows the use of large plant that is better able to meet faster construction objectives, within the overall constraints of access and site size.

Pre-stressed or tensioned members. Identify and plan any removal to avoid delays to the programme caused by unexpected demolition of tensioned members (**see CIRIA TN129** *Pre-stressed concrete beams, controlled demolition and pre-stress loss assessment*).

4.1.3 Foundations

When building foundations faster construction can be achieved by the following:

Consider whether piling is necessary. Decide whether it will enable an earlier start to be made on subsequent construction. Piling is perceived as a relatively fast activity, but it can occupy part of the site and hold up following trades. It also occupies specialised operatives who are then prevented from carrying out other activities on the site.

Reduce the number of piles, eg by using fewer but larger piles. Investigate the availability of the latest plant that might allow larger or deeper piles to be designed. Alternatively, consider the benefits of using a larger number of smaller piles. The duration of activity is determined by the nature of the site, the type of piling rig used, and the number of piles to be installed.

Over-design so that working piles can continue to be installed during the pile test. It may be possible to construct working piles during the pile test by increasing the pile length or diameter.

Pile from ground level with "blind bore" (empty) for depth of substructure. This allows all piling to be formed from a ground-level platform by the piling rig(s). It avoids the need for ramps, temporary works or return visits to pile at a lower level after excavation for substructure.

Design permanent foundations to be used as tower crane bases. Tower crane bases that are within the footprint of the structure can be constructed at a level and location to form a foundation, or part of one. This allows the permanent works above to progress instead of having to wait for any omitted foundations. Tower cranes can also be founded within the permanent works above ground level.

Comprehensive ground information. Ensure a thorough site investigation survey is undertaken to reduce the risk of unforeseen ground conditions. The detail of this should be weighed against the cost of rectifying likely problems that might occur with a shallower, less detailed survey, eg swallow holes in chalk area, unknown contaminated ground or having to move location due to an obstruction. If the result is out of specification, consider how the design needs to be modified to allow construction to remain on programme (**ICE** *Inadequate site investigation*; **AD Robb** *Site investigation*).

Ease and speed of constructing mass foundations. For example, raft versus piling. It might be more advantageous overall to choose the quickest option rather than the cheapest.

Site access. Ensure that the foundation construction method allows good site access to be maintained.

Temporary works. Ensure that propping or supports for temporary works do not hinder site access. Cantilevered walls might be a better solution than props (**see CIRIA SP95** *Design and construction of sheet piled cofferdams*).

Concrete mixes. Use of standard concrete mixes will reduce or avoid the need for

advance testing with trial mixes. Compare the cost of over-design with the cost of spending more time on extra design, testing and control (**see CIRIA R165** *The planning and design of concrete mixes for transporting, placing and finishing*).

Concrete construction. Cast concrete against earth, depending on the soil condition (if it includes reinforcement, add extra cover), or use back blinding to reduce the need for shuttering.

Bulk supply and cart away. Identify if vehicle access to and from the site, and on site, is the limiting factor for the fast supply or removal of material.

Ready-mixed concrete access. Consider providing access for ready-mixed concrete trucks to drive up to large pours for concrete placement. Other options include the use of skips, pumps, conveyors or chutes.

Concrete compaction. Choosing concrete vibration or self-compacting concrete for optimum speed of placement.

Concreting in water or bad ground. Tremmie concrete can be used where there are severe water or ground support problems, instead of attempting major de-watering operations or employing propping systems.

Large concrete pours. Large concrete pours reduce the need to prepare construction joints. Allowance should be made for the effects of higher temperatures caused by the heat of hydration of the cement. Consider the need for cooling, use of additives or addition of slag to the concrete mix (**see CIRIA R135** *Concreting deep lifts and large volume pours*; **R49** *Large concrete pours – a survey of current practice*).

Concrete additives. Consider the use of additives to the concrete mix when fast pouring, especially in hot or cold climatic conditions.

General reference. See CIRIA SP136 *Site guide to foundation construction.*

4.1.4 Substructure

Faster construction during substructure construction can be achieved by the following:

Below-ground work. Avoid below-ground work if possible – "If it's formed below, it's slow".

Temporary works. The cost of leaving steel sheet piles in position might be offset by avoiding the expense and time involved in withdrawing them.

Incorporate temporary works solutions in permanent works. The temporary works solution can act as permanent structure. For example, a diaphragm/secant pile wall can be used as an earth support in place of sheet piles or open cut.

Avoid propping of temporary works intruding into the site. Use retaining structures that do not require intrusive propping while in the temporary condition. Alternatives include cantilever sheet piles and ground anchors. Where possible, avoid temporary works propping.

Top-down construction. Use top-down construction for a substructure combined or overlapped with superstructure construction, for example (check ventilation and muck-away routes)

De-watering advantages in appropriate soil conditions. Some easily drained soils allow better working conditions that are appropriate for faster construction techniques. In granular materials, for example, well-points can be sunk away from the workface to lower the local water table, to give dry working conditions. On the other hand, clay, which drains less freely and is relatively impermeable, might help conditions by keeping water away from an excavation. In water-logged impermeable soils, de-watering might involve over-excavation and back-filling with a draining material, or constructing a sheet-piled coffer-dam to cut off the water.

Undercrofts for below-slab services. Consider constructing undercrofts for below-slab services, rather than excavating ground for trenches and buried services. If large areas of dense below-ground services are on a critical part of the programme, it may be preferable to design an undercroft to be constructed in the substructure part of the programme of work.

Prefabrication of services. Prefabricate off site those services that are to be buried or cast-in, to avoid protracted workface activities, especially for complicated details in manholes, for example.

Prefabricate reinforcement cages/mats. Deliver prefabricated cages or mats of reinforcement to the workface. This improves accuracy for immediate positioning into the pour area.

Avoid small-diameter reinforcement. Use reinforcement of 16 mm diameter or larger if staff need to walk on the mats.

Standard concrete finishes. Avoid quality concrete finishes and the need for watertight construction by using inner-skin walls with drainage channels.

Design construction joints to be easily and quickly prepared. This usually means not using concrete scabbling. It might mean the use of concrete formwork retarders and laitence removal with wire brushes or water/air lines **(see CIRIA R146 *Design and construction of joints in concrete structures*).**

Avoid the use of water-bars. Avoid the use of water-bars, if possible, because they slow the concreting preparation process. Increasing the concrete interface width might be an alternative. If they have to be used, surface water-bars fixed to the formwork might prove a faster option.

4.1.5 Superstructure

Faster construction during superstructure construction can be achieved by the following:

Slip/jump-form lift shafts. Concrete slip-forming is generally faster for continuous vertical concrete shafts or cores and might also be able to be used for horizontal slips.

Tilt-up construction. Consider the use of build and lift-up construction, such as panel-type systems that form wall panels.

Steel frame structures. Although steel frame structures are often the fastest to erect, their use must be looked at in the context of the whole structure. Points to consider include corrosion protection and the need for protection against fire. It might be possible to save time by applying the protection off site in the fabrication works.

Off-site welding. Avoid on-site welding, especially for small applications, because it requires a careful quality regime to be set up, which is unlikely to contribute to faster construction. In a controlled on-site regime, welding can be a fast system of connection, but any benefits must be weighed against the time penalties involved in set-up and control.

Extra material/labour hoists to provide adequate access and supply. Site progress should not be dictated by the speed and volume of the material or plant supplied to the workface simply because of inadequate horizontal or vertical transportation on site.

Metal decking for slabs as permanent forms. This is now a well used and accepted method of providing fast permanent formwork to slab soffits and avoids the consideration of striking times. Decking that also provides reinforcement offers double benefit where fire protection is not required or is provided by a ceiling liner.

Special-purpose slab/beam stop-ends. These may be provided for fixing to metal decking as stop-ends for slabs or beams as permanent formwork.

Table-forms. This system of combined falsework and formwork for fast construction of concrete beam and slab construction is most effective where floor plates repeat several times above each other. It can also be used where there is little variation in floor heights (there is still scope for accommodating some variation in height, however).

Precast elements; deck slabs/precast columns. Casting elements away from the workface, either in a remote factory or elsewhere on the site, can provide substantial productivity and efficiency gains. The great benefit is the ability to produce elements without interfering with critical site production. The volume of production is less likely to be a critical path programme function and quality will be substantially higher because of the controlled production environment. Other potential benefits include increased output, lower cost and improved safety.

Concrete permanent slab forms for composite concrete construction. Concrete planks or slabs can be used as soffit permanent forms, which might also improve structural behaviour because the building is able to function as a composite structure.

Pumpable concrete mixes/concrete pumps. This is often an essential element for faster construction because the concrete pump frees up the tower cranes during concreting for other activities **(see CIRIA R165 *The planning and design of concrete mixes for transporting, placing and finishing*).**

High early-strength concrete. Although probably more expensive to provide, high early-strength concrete allows early access on to the concrete structure and progression of subsequent structures. Consideration might have to be given to dealing with increased heat of hydration **(see CIRIA R136 *Formwork striking times – criteria, prediction and methods of assessment*).**

Spray-curing of concrete. Spray-curing can be applied immediately after concreting top surfaces and upon striking formed surfaces. It has the advantage that it can almost immediately be walked upon, allowing early safe access on to the concrete structure. Although theoretically less efficient than other membranes, it is easily applied correctly and only once.

Push-pull propping for walls or column shutter boxes. Reduces the number of props used and avoids operatives working at edge conditions.

Assess the capability of locally available plant. This is especially relevant when projects are being built overseas. Consider, for example, that plant limitations might mean that large sections cannot be handled so easily and therefore quickly.

Use standard steel sections and quality. These are more likely to be readily available, avoiding the risk of long procurement and lead-in times.

Early pre-order curved or welded built-up steel sections. Such elements are likely to be on long order and require specialist fabricators that may not be available locally or when required.

Dry-lining for fire protection. Avoid all wet trades. However, if wet trades are to be used, ensure that these activities do not have hidden effects on adjacent or subsequent trades. Do not forget to allow for curing times. Also assess the possible effect on the surrounding environment, such as areas for the general public.

Reinforcement installation with prefabricated reinforcement cages/mats. Have prefabricated cages or mats of reinforcement delivered to the workface. This allows immediate positioning into the pour area.

Consider speed and capacity of cranes on site. Cranes need not always be designed for the heaviest or largest loads required. For the majority of lifts, smaller cranes may be faster. Use mobile cranes for the biggest lifts **(see CIRIA SP131 *Crane stability on site*).**

Avoiding site painting of steelwork. Site painting usually sterilises areas of the site, preventing other activities progressing simultaneously and subsequently during the drying and protection activity period. Invariably the quality of finish is inferior to factory-finished work. **(see CIRIA R174 *New paint systems for the protection of construction steelwork*).**

Use structural props. Place these directly on to the soffit of poured concrete spans to allow early striking of forms and falsework, leaving the structural props to offer further support while the concrete gains strength.

Avoid reworking on adjacent work. The pollution and disturbance created on site by any material may inhibit faster construction. Protection may be necessary on architectural finishes to minimise rework and its effect on the programmed procedures. For example, cement-based sprayed protection may be a fast and economical solution to fire protection, but if adjacent trades have not allowed for application and clean-up, the overall programme may lengthen. Welding adjacent to glass causes similar problems, and protecting the glass from weld spatter is preferable to removing and replacing window units.

4.1.6 Cladding

Faster construction during cladding will be achieved by the following:

Self-erecting or secondary craneage systems. Use self-erecting or secondary craneage systems that do not rely on main site craneage. This allows tower cranes to be used for other activities.

Tilt-up panel system. Build or site-assemble and tilt-up construction may be in panel-type systems that form wall-cladding panels.

Large ready-glazed units, truss panels. Cladding can be attached to a structure as panels on a truss panel. A truss panel accommodates several cladding units and can be lifted onto the building and fixed as a truss panel. The process allows a large area of cladding to be assembled on the building façade quickly, achieving water-tightness very fast.

Tolerances. Ensure tolerances are compatible and generous with building structure and adjacent trades. The project as a whole must have compatible tolerances. Little will be achieved if cladding panels with small tolerances are fixed to a frame with large tolerances that lacks flexibility in the fixings to accommodate the different tolerances.

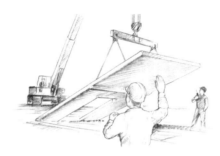

Use simple fixings/simple and fast cladding connections to the structure/frame. The design of fast and simple fixings precludes the use of details such as cast-in starter bars and fixings that have no tolerance for adjustment once the cladding is secured on to the building. Such details may involve drilled-in fixings that can only be made once the exact location is known. Also they may require cladding panels to be held on the crane hook for long periods to obtain the correct positioning of the panel. The key is to have cladding fixing details that allow the panel to be secured to the building accurately in a few seconds, releasing the crane for other lifts and involving operatives at the building edge for the minimum time. The panel can then be adjusted and checked in the knowledge that the cladding is secure. Ensure, then, that cladding fixing for panel security does not remove adjustment for line and level, and that line and level adjustment of the panel is not reliant on crane hook attendance.

Use reliable fixings and provide spares. Use fixings that are reliable in their own operation and can be fixed successfully into the anchoring material. Avoid having to

delay release from the crane hook in order to test whether the panel is secure.

Colour-match adjacent units before site assembly. Ensure that colour matching of panels is carried out before they are fixed on the building. This is especially important where the cladding panels are in natural materials such as stone or timber. Aesthetic debate can be held in the fabrication yard where the activity is off the critical path for faster panel erection.

Avoid hand-fixed stone cladding. Hand-fixed stone is a craftsman's job and is likely to be very slow. Alternatively, ensure that sufficient labour is available for hand-fixing stone cladding so that it is not a critical activity.

Fabricate stone cladding in trusses or panels. Hand-fix the stone in truss panels off site or away from the workface area, thereby removing the activity from the programme's critical path.

Locate cladding fixings inboard from building edge. Assist faster construction by locating cladding fixings for panels well inboard from the edge of the structure when in their final position. The operatives fixing the panels will feel more comfortable working away from the edge of the structure, even though they will still be on safety lines. It might even be possible to arrange the details so that operatives work behind handrails.

Use dry gaskets everywhere. Install a cladding system that does not use a wet system of mastic jointing. For faster construction this has the double advantage that dry gaskets can be fixed in poor weather conditions (provided it is safe to do so) and do not rely on continued good conditions for the curing of sealant.

Provide internal access to glazing panels if glass size permits. Internal access for glazing of cladding panels is quicker and therefore safer, provided the glass panels are of a size that allows them to be transported through the building. Cladding panels may arrive at the workface already glazed. In that situation, design will need to consider maintenance procedures, especially ongoing access to the inside and outside of the façade as well as the size of the glazing panels.

Avoid one-off panels. Avoid the design and use of one-off panel types, ie use ten each of ten types, not 90 of one type plus ten different one-offs. This largely removes the risk of delaying panel erection through error, damage or non-delivery of panels.

Avoid fitting rain screen on site. Ensure that rain screens are fitted in the cladding fabrication works. The risk of damage to a site-fitted rain screen is too high, especially where construction is fast.

Optimise crane cladding panel off-loading times. If crane hook time is at a premium, consider crane off-loading at night or installing cladding panels at weekends.

Ensure correct cladding panel delivery sequence. Deliver cladding panels in the order they are to be placed on the building or structure, and just in time.

Cladding panel lifting. Use cladding panel lifting points or handling cradle; never use slings. Slings are too slow and are easily trapped under the lift, causing delay.

4.1.7 Services

Faster construction during services installation can be achieved by the following:

Optimise with off-site plant and services fabrication and pre-assembly. This avoids assembly time at the workface and delay to following activities. Ensure that an assembled unit can be located on site. This includes weight lift considerations and access restraints.

Plant rooms in basements. Early installation of plant and equipment in the completed basement building structure allows an early start to plant installation, thus shortening the programme. Careful consideration must be given to plant access for maintenance and replacement. Also watertightness must be achieved to avoid damage to plant and equipment.

Allow enough space under suspended floor and above false ceiling voids. This facilitates and speeds installation of services. An opportunity also exists for a good layout discipline.

Phase testing and commissioning of partial systems. Early partial commissioning of phases of services provides early knowledge of results, good or bad, and lessens the effect on the fast programme.

Commission lifts early. This enables early occupation or use by the finishing trade or commissioning engineers. Protection to the lift-car is necessary. Agreement must first be obtained from the client, designer and lift manufacturer.

Use of communal facilities for services. Eg cable pits, between suppliers.

Flexibility in suppliers' delivery programmes. Suppliers need to be flexible on their delivery programmes to respond to progress by others.

Flexibility in installer's programme of delivered plant and equipment. Installers need to be flexible on their installation programmes to respond to progress by suppliers. Do everything possible to keep long-lead order items off the programme critical path.

Check reliability of key existing cable/pipe locations. Assess the reliability of historical information. Note the age of information and services, depth recorded and likely amendments since then. Programme work according to likely disruptions and resurvey the area if appropriate.

Use ceiling and floor voids as plenums. Use ceiling and floor voids as plenums to reduce ductwork installation.

Avoid site-fixed cast-in services. Put services into stud-work partitions or surface-fix, place below raised floors and above suspended ceilings.

Use modular and prefabricated wiring harnesses. In structured services layouts, or where there is a high degree of repetition, modular and prefabricated wiring harnesses may be designed and used to speed installation. The harnesses are located into position and plugged in, the wiring connections having already been made and tested in a controlled environment.

Use a soffit channel grid system. Above a heavily serviced area, a channel grid system cast into the concrete soffit or fixed to the structure provides support for hung services on the basis of a common fixing for all trades. The channel grid system can be uni-directional or a grid at right-angles. The hangers may also provide hangers to support false ceilings as well as lighting.

Specify equipment that is a standard item. Specifying plant and equipment that are standard and have a short delivery times not only reduces the risk of late supply, but limits the effect of reordering if equipment is damaged during faster construction.

Specify lightweight, easy-to-assemble materials. Operatives can locate and position items more easily and therefore faster.

Zone service routes. Zone service routes so that each discipline has its own level and corridor of space.

Vertical and horizontal services distribution. Vertical and horizontal services distribution should be collective and fixed in collective routes, not fixed randomly.

Builders' work. Identify all builders' work hole requirements on the structural drawings. This demands close co-ordination between the structural and services designer, architect and builder. Avoid the need for post-constructional drilling of holes for builders' work details. Use computer visualisation to check clashes.

4.1.8 Finishes

When applying the finishes, faster construction can be achieved by the following:

Complete in "zones" to enable early occupation of lower floors. If work is completed in carefully planned zones, clients may be able to take early beneficial occupation without the associated contractual problems of occupying areas that are incomplete and the subsequent compromise to warranties.

Use simple and reliable fixings. Employ simple fixings that are quick and easy to use and either allow locational adjustment or locate the element.

Ensure batches are compatible. Avoid matching materials on site with selection off site in controlled conditions. Matching selection is likely to be subjective anyway and takes considerable time. This slow activity on site is not conducive to faster construction. Carry out matching at the works or factory.

Ease of application: crane, scaffold, hoist. Consider the activities necessary to get the materials into their final location as a fast delivery activity.

Avoid applications that sterilise an area. Avoid applications that sterilise an area to other trades or the public during application and/or curing periods, eg spray paint, mastic application.

Use dry finish applications. Use a dry finish application, eg sheet material, rather than a site-applied spray finish that requires the application areas to be isolated and needs a curing period before surface protection can take place and operatives can engage in subsequent activities.

Sequence trades to avoid damage. Keep activity away from finished surfaces, even when they are protected. Towards the end of the project, finishes will be unprotected, but operatives will still be working quickly.

Apply finishes off site. This improves quality and avoids additional site activities; eg doors arrive on site already hung on frames with applied finishes and temporary protection.

Create clean zones of finished work. Create clean zones of finished work areas. Issue permits to enter the system and provide protective clothing. Plan site activities to work away from finished areas. Faster construction programmes will not accommodate significant site traffic through areas of finished surfaces.

Protect finishes. Protect finishes to avoid the need for repair or replacement. Protection should be appropriate to the need. Protection for transportation may be substantially different to that required for protection from site activities. Protection should be designed to avoid the need for its removal during installation on site.

Transportation and handling of finished surfaces. Transport and handle finished surfaces with care. A careless action or inadequate protection may cause significant delays.

Early installation of raised floors. Put in raised floors to protect floor void services from site traffic. Lay finish to raised floor later if the system permits, or protect the raised floor finish from site traffic.

Avoid large or heavy elements that have applied finishes. Handling difficulties increase the risk of damage. Use smaller elements or clad with finishes later. The design should take into account abnormal construction loading requirements on the raised floor.

Purchase spare elements. Buy sufficient finished spare elements to be able to replace damaged work on site without affecting site production rates and the faster construction programme. At the end of the construction consider handing on surplus elements to the facilities manager.

4.2 Case study examples

Case Study 1

Celcon Thin Joint System

History

H & H Celcon Ltd launched the use of its thin joint mortar system in 1998. The main elements of the system are the thin joint mortar, branded Celfix. This fast-setting strong mortar can be easily applied in a thin layer (2–3 mm).

Mortar

Celfix mortar has been produced to complement the overall performance of the blocks and improve productivity so that it is possible to build the supporting structure of a house in days. The mortar is a cement-based product supplied as a dry pre-mixed powder in 25 kg bags. The mortar formulation has been designed to start setting within ten minutes of mixing with the required amount of water and is applied using a notched scoop.

Celcon Jumbo Units

Although traditional-format blocks can be used for thin joint blockwork, the larger units, typically measuring 440 mm x 430 mm high, optimises the mortar's productivity benefits. The Jumbo unit equates to two and a half traditional-sized blocks, or almost 15 bricks.

Productivity

The quick bonding time of the mortar reduces the effect of the weight of masonry squeezing out wet mortar on lower courses, enabling greater wall heights to be built in a day. The strength of bond achieved allows the floors and roof to be installed the following day. Rates have been quoted at 100 m² a day for each bricklayer and rates of up to 25 m²/h with traditional-format blocks.

The accuracy and consistency of the mortar joint thickness reduces time spent levelling and gauging courses. Where external walls are of cavity construction, the inner leaf can be built first, enabling easier inspection of work, and easier fixing of any additional insulation. This also allows internal trades to work while the external skin is constructed. Extra productivity can also be obtained from the use of thin coat spray plaster finishes. These finishes can only be used where the accuracy of construction is similar to that achieved by thin joint blockwork.

(See 3.3.2, 4.1.5)

Case Study 2

K'Nex Fire Sprinkler Tank Relocation Project – Ashford

The existing sprinkler tank at the K'Nex site was directly on the alignment of the Channel Tunnel Rail Link. It needed to be relocated in order not to obstruct the progress of the Rail Link construction. The project involved the design, procurement and construction of the new tank foundations, water tank, adjacent single-storey pump house with pumps, and diesel tank room with tank. To meet Union Railways Property's very fast programme, the construction had to be completed in nine weeks.

A masonry block retaining wall was constructed around the site. The pumped sprinkler pipe-work, mains pipe-work and electrical services were re-routed from the existing sprinkler tank location to the location of the new tanks and pumps. The ground-bearing bases to the sprinkler tank, pump and diesel tank rooms were constructed in reinforced concrete.

The sprinkler tank was clad in a profiled metal cladding. Brickwork walling was used for the pump house and diesel tank room. The pump-house has a concrete roof slab. Interconnecting pipe-work was above and below ground. The design of the tank and pumps incorporated standard components where possible to minimise design, procurement and installation times.

To allow the construction periods on site to be achieved, the project manager advised the client that it should pre-order all the large plant that had long procurement periods, to which the client agreed. The plant was novated to the main contractor, RJ Barwick & Sons Ltd, as soon as it was appointed. This allowed construction of the new pumping station on site to progress in accordance with the fast programme and to be operational in time for the Rail Link alignment contract.

The project was satisfactorily completed and there were no residual situations from the project that were not known or anticipated in the design and construction.

(See 3.2.1, 4.1.6)

This case study demonstrates that:

- traditional building activities can be speeded up
- the benefits of improvements to existing materials
- use of larger elements increases productivity.

This case study demonstrates the benefits of:

- clear brief from the client to achieve fast construction on site
- incorporation of standard components
- decisive action taken on pre-ordering of plant.

Case Study 3
Road replacement

Research in West Sussex by road surfacing specialist Colas concluded that if the waste road material dug out during road replacement was recycled it would save the client money, reduce on-site times and energy costs, and reduce the environmental impacts of importing new material and landfilling the waste.

A few years ago, Colas carried out a pilot scheme to rebuild a primary road with in-depth recycling. The scheme was appraised and approved by the Transport Research Laboratory, Epsom & Ewell Council (Surrey) and consultant WS Atkins. They identified a potential saving of up to 30 per cent on price, as well as time savings and several energy and environmental benefits over more conventional repairs. There was:

- no wasteful excavation and disposal to tip
- reduction in the use of new materials
- reduced energy, fuel and haulage costs
- reduced time on site and noise nuisance.

Where appropriate, trial holes and cores are taken to determine the make-up of the road. After the traffic data are assessed, the depth of road to be recycled is agreed. For example, if the total structure of the road has failed, full in-depth recycling down to 450 mm is proposed. However, if the base course layer has failed and the road is lightly trafficked, then only 75 mm is pulverised ("retread"). For a failed wearing course, only the top 34–40 mm is recycled ("repave").

Surrey County Council has monitored both the repave and retread recycling operations piloted by Colas, and opted for a term contract using those systems for the structural maintenance of all country roads. This type of work had previously been tendered piecemeal.

(See 3.3.2)

Case Study 4
Asda Superstore, Wembley

Partnering between Tarmac, Laing, HBG, Pearce and Asda began in 1995. Since then, the time taken to construct a standard Asda superstore has been reduced by 45 per cent. A recent store at Wembley was handed over within 19 weeks and opened for trading 20 weeks from start of steel frame erection.

Key factors contributing to this success included:

- familiarisation of product through repeat projects
- partnering with supply chain
- continuous improvement forums for same and mixed disciplinary groups
- incentivisation
- client commitment to improvement
- client commitment to innovation
- a philosophy of stretching targets
- risks rest with appropriate party.

Performance is also monitored and improved in areas such as safety, quality, cost saving and customer satisfaction.

Broad issues seen as key within the construction process include:

- planning – both at the outset and ongoing
- management of the flow and quality of design information
- input and early involvement by the whole team in buildability and methodology
- management of change.

(See 3.2.1)

This case study demonstrates that:
- innovative road repair solutions mean faster construction on site
- improved environmental and sustainability performance can be achieved
- the benefit of less waste and shorter road closures can be achieved

---

This case study demonstrated the benefits of:
- early involvement of key package contractors
- "make ready" analysis and action for key activities
- all actions challenged for optimum performance
- ensuring all involved understand the performance required individually and as a team.

Case Study 5

Toyota (GB) Limited new headquarters, Epsom, Surrey

Recent research by Oxford Brookes University and the University of Salford concluded that hybrid structures could bring about faster construction on site. Other benefits were cheaper construction, greater accuracy, reduced environmental impact, lower incidence of site accidents and greater thermal capacity.

The architectural concept at Epsom is based on four office wings radiating from a glazed street, which houses all communal facilities and connects to an entrance rotunda. The office structure is a hybrid structure using precast concrete columns and coffered floor and roof units with in-situ concrete beams and floor screed to provide structural integrity.

The client's brief and its interpretation by the architects, allowed the principles of hybrid construction to be applied. The exposed structure was required to have a high-quality finish. After the alternatives had been studied for faster construction, the hybrid precast solution was the logical choice, particularly when combined with a need for snag-free construction.

Trent Concrete won the contract for the manufacture at works and the supply of circular columns up to 8 m high and 500 mm in diameter. Floor units were 3 m wide and 6 m long, and featured a complex coffered soffit. All units were cast in glass-fibre-lined moulds in order to produce the high-quality ex-mould finish that was specified to avoid the need for further decoration. This avoided the need for a further trade and reduced maintenance over the life of the building. The exposed concrete surfaces also provide greater thermal capacity, contributing positively to the building energy management. This helped to achieve a low-cost energy policy on site in assembly and in operational use throughout the occupied life of the building.

(See 3.3.1, 4.1.5)

This case study demonstrates the benefits of:

- correct interpretation of the client's brief
- early decisions on construction method-related design
- efforts to reduce or eliminate tracks on the critical path.

Case Study 6

Project NG4-F, Rover Group, Hams Hall

The project called for the construction of a 300 m-long, 20 m - wide, 7m deep integral service trench below the basement within the new engine factory. Four construction options were considered, which would have a direct bearing on the final design of the trench:

1. Construction of a conventional reinforced concrete retaining wall in situ in open cut.
2. Construction of RC secant bored pile wall in part open cut from a reduced level. Basement continuing using bottom-up construction.
3. Construction of RC secant bored pile wall from existing ground level. Basement continuing using bottom-up construction.
4. Construction of RC secant bored pile wall from existing ground level. Basement continuing using top-down construction.

Due to the depth of the cofferdam Option 1 was not considered further. Options 2 and 3 were designed and costed in some detail. Option 4 was the preferred option to achieve the optimum programme benefits.

The detailed design of the top-down method of construction incorporated a central line of plunged columns that would provide the structural steelwork for the overlying building frame. These columns were installed to steelwork tolerances. The cofferdam was designed to act as a full cantilever as well as part-propped to allow the excavation sequence to match the contractor's programme. 300 tension piles were installed from ground level within the cofferdam footprint to prevent base heave during excavation.

To meet the very tight contract programme, five specialised piling rigs and three crawler cranes were required. A dedicated slurry batching plant was also built of sufficient size to serve all rigs.

Team working was instituted on the project, and individuals were empowered and encouraged to make active decisions that would achieve the programme and improve the quality of their work.

Following the cofferdam excavation and exposure of internal plunged columns, the work was recorded as being well within the specified tolerances. There was no delay recorded to any concurrent work or follow-on trades.

(See 4.1.3)

This case study demonstrates the benefit of:

- considering several construction method options
- early consideration of resources required on site
- team working and active decision-making.

4.3 References

Atkinson, A, Cavilla, J and Wells, J. *Securing the Contractor's Contribution to Buildability in Design*, Project Report 27 (London: CIRIA, 1997, ISBN 0 86017 827 7)

Bamforth, P B and Price, W F. *Concreting deep lifts and large volume pours,* Report 135 (London: CIRIA, 1995, ISBN 0 86017 420 4)

Bennett, D F H and Gordon R W. *Project Profiles, Broadwalk House*, Publication 97.313 (British Cement Association, 1990, ISBN 0 7210 1388 0)

Bielby, S C. *Site safety handbook (3rd edn)*, Special Publication 151 (London: CIRIA, 2001, ISBN 0 86017 800 5)

Birt, J C. *Large concrete pours – a survey of current practice*, Report 49 (London: CIRIA, 1974, ISBN 0 901208 81 7)

Bussell, M N and Cather, R. *Design and construction of joints in concrete structures,* Report 146 (London: CIRIA, 1995, ISBN 0 86017 429 8)

CIRIA. *Alternative Tendering Initiative – March 1995*, CPN Note 4 (London: CIRIA, 1995)

CIRIA. *Single Project Modelling*, CPN Note 6 (London: CIRIA, 1995)

CIRIA. *Time compression programme*, CPN Note 7 (London: CIRIA, 1995)

CIRIA. *Taking Latham forward through procurement-led initiatives*, CPN Note 37 (London: CIRIA, 1996)

CIRIA. *Delivering better construction performance – the influence of design on site productivity*, CPN Note 39 (London: CIRIA, 1996)

CIRIA. *Handbook of supply chain management. The essentials*, Report C546, (London; CIRIA, 2000. ISBN 0 86017 546 4)

Considerate Constructors Scheme. *Code of practice.* (Considerate Constructors Scheme. 1997-, http://www.ccscheme.org.uk)

Construction Task Force. *Rethinking Construction,* Egan, J, Chairman, DETR, 1998

Coventry, S and Guthrie, P. *Waste minimisation and recycling in construction – design manual,* Special Publication 134 (London: CIRIA, 1998, ISBN 0 86017 500 6)

Gedge, G and Whitehouse, N. *New paint systems for the protection of construction steelwork*, Report 174 (London: CIRIA, 1997, ISBN 0 86017 472 7)

Goodchild, C H. *Hybrid Concrete Construction*, Publication 97.337 (British Cement Association, 1995)

Guthrie, P, Woolveridge, C and Coventry, S. *Managing materials and components on site*, Special Publication 146 (London: CIRIA, 1998, ISBN 0 86017 481 6)

Guthrie, P M, Woolveridge, A C and Patel, V S. *Waste minimisation in construction – site guide*, Special Publication 133 (London: CIRIA, 1997, ISBN 0 86017 482 4)

Harris, M R et al. *Remedial treatment for contaminated land (Vols I–XII)*, Special Publications 101–112 (London: CIRIA, 1995–8)

Harris, M R, Herbert, S M and Smith, M A. *Remedial treatment for contaminated land Vol II – decommissioning, decontamination and demolition,* Special Publication 102 (London: CIRIA, 1995, ISBN 0 86017 397 6)

Harrison, T A. *Formwork striking times – criteria, prediction and methods of assessment*, Report 136 (London: CIRIA, 1995, ISBN 0 86017 431 X)

Institution of Civil Engineers. *Inadequate site investigation.* (London: Thomas telford, 1991. ISBN 07277 1645 X)

Key Performance Indicators, Construction Best Practice Programme (DETR, 1999)

Latham, Sir Michael. "Constructing the team", *Construction Industry Review,* July 1994 (London: HMSO, ISBN 0 11 752994 X)

Lindsell, P and Buchner, S H. *Prestressed concrete beams: controlled demolition and prestress loss assessment*, Technical Note 129 (London: CIRIA, 1987, ISBN 0 86017 277 5)

Lloyd, D (ed). *Crane stability on site: an introductory guide*, Special Publication 131 (London: CIRIA, 1996, ISBN 0 86017 456 5)

Lloyd, D and Kay, T. *Temporary access to the workface: a handbook for young professionals*, Special Publication 121 (London: CIRIA, 1995, ISBN 0 86017 422 0)

Martin, W S. *Site guide to foundation construction – a handbook for young professionals*, Special Publication 136 (London: CIRIA, 1996, ISBN 0 86017 459 X)

Masterton, G G T and Wilson, R A. *The planning and design of concrete mixes for transporting, placing and finishing,* Report 165 (London: CIRIA, 1997, ISBN 0 86017 470 0)

Ove Arup & Partners. *CDM Regulations – work sector guidance for designers*, Report 166 (London: CIRIA, 1997, ISBN 0 86017 464 6)

Pickrell, S, Garnett, N and Baldwin, J. *"Measuring up" – A practical guide to benchmarking in construction* (Construction Research Communications Ltd, 1997, ISBN 1 86081 1817)

Potter, M. *Planning to build? A practical introduction to the construction process*, Special Publication 113 (London: CIRIA, 1995, ISBN 0 86017 433 6)

Robb, AD. *Site investigation.* (London: Thomas Telford, 1982. ISBN 0 7277 0142 8)

Sadgrove, B M. *Setting-out procedures* (2nd edn), Special Publication 145 (London: CIRIA, 1997, ISBN 0 86017 478 6)

Southcott, M F and Tovey, A K. *Tilt-up Concrete Buildings: Design and Construction Guide,* Publication 97.366 (British Cement Association, 1998, ISBN 0 7210 1533 6)

Sparkman, G, Groák, S, Gibb, A and Neale, R. *Standardisation and pre-assembly – adding value to construction projects,* Report 176 (London: CIRIA, 1999, ISBN 0 86017 498 0)

Steeds, J E, Shepherd, E and Barry, D L. *A guide for safe working practices for contaminated sites*, Report 132 and Special Publication 119 (London: CIRIA, 1996, ISBN 0 86017 451 4)

Williams, B and Waite, D. *The design and construction of sheet-piled cofferdams*, Special Publication 95 (London: CIRIA, 1993, ISBN 0 86017 361 5)

Wills, A J and Churcher, D W. *How much noise do you make? A guide to assessing and managing noise on construction sites*, Project Report 70 (London: CIRIA, 1999, ISBN 0 86017 870 6)

Visual assessment chart template

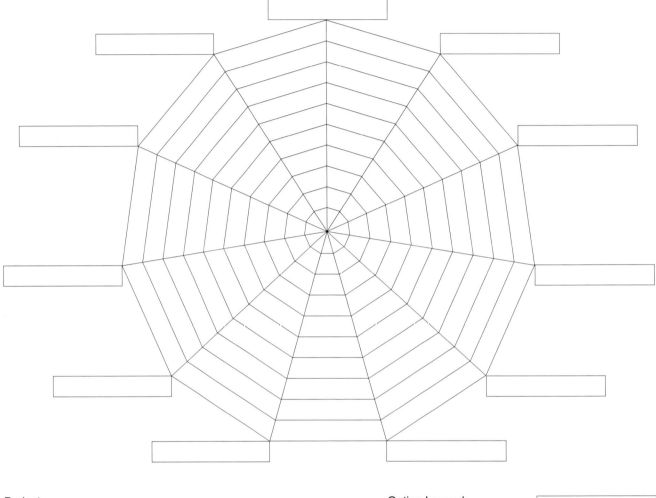

Project:

Stage

Option Legend: